A QUEST FOR
MORE

Living for something
bigger than you

PAUL DAVID TRIPP

www.newgrowthpress.com

Prolific author and international conference speaker, Paul David Tripp, is president of Paul Tripp Ministries, whose mission is to educate and equip today's Christian by combining the in-depth study of God's Word with practical life application. Tripp, also a pastor with over 15 years of pastoral ministry, is an adjunct professor at Westminster Theological Seminary and adjunct faculty member at the Christian Counseling & Educational Foundation in Glenside, Pennsylvania. He is the author of such best-selling titles as *Instruments in the Redeemer's Hands, War of Words, Age of Opportunity, Lost in the Middle, How People Change,* and *Relationships: A Mess Worth Making.* Tripp has been married for 35 years and has four grown children.

New Growth Press, Greensboro 27404
© 2007, 2008 by Paul David Tripp
All rights reserved. Published 2008
15 14 13 12 11 10 09 08   6 5 4 3 2

Cover Design: Ethan Tripp
Interior Design: The DesignWorks Group, www.thedesignworksgroup.com
Typesetting: Blackbird Creative, www.blackbirdcreative.biz
Photo of Paul Tripp: David Sacks, www.davidsacks.com

ISBN-10: 0-9785567-4-7
ISBN-13: 978-0-9785567-4-7

Library of Congress Control Number: 2007933626

Printed in Canada

None of what this book represents would be possible without the many people who over the years have been my teachers, mentors, examples, helpers, and friends. I thank God for you and your contribution to what God has called me to do.

CONTENTS

PREFACE

Some books are a concentrated examination of a topic. Other books lay out a set of skills or techniques for a certain aspect of life. Some books record a person's experience or journey. Others are funny or sad.

The book you are about to read doesn't fit into any of these categories.

Here is my best attempt to tell you what you are about to read: This entire book is meant to stimulate you to think about one central biblical concept, the kingdom of God. But this book is not a theology of kingdom, nor an exposition of the kingdom passages in the Bible. No, it is simply a meditation on what Jesus meant when he called us to "seek first his kingdom." What does it really look like to expand everything our lives contain to touch the size of his kingdom?

Now, the problem with biblical terms like "kingdom" is that they are familiar-but-unfamiliar terms. It is quite possible for us to have heard them many times and even used them in our own conversations, yet not to really understand what they mean. Or we may know technically what they mean, but not how they set the agenda for the way we live every day.

The discussion of kingdom living in this book will not take place in the seminary hallway. I am going to take you to the street where the rubber meets the road in daily life. I want to help you consider Christ's call from the street level. And my hope is that, as we do this together, you will first become uncomfortable, but then soon become encouraged, excited, and motivated with hope.

God has given you the gift of his Son, not to make your little kingdom successful, but to welcome you to a much better kingdom. Now what in the world does that mean?

PAUL DAVID TRIPP

INTRODUCTION

A WORD ABOUT THE JOURNEY

Reading is much like a long journey. You are excited in the beginning, simply because you are getting started. Anticipation is a motivating thing. But it isn't long before the journey begins to feel longer than you thought it would. Midway through your trip, you just can't wait for indications that the end is near. You begin to celebrate when you see the sign that tells you that you have only a few miles to go.

This book is like a journey, but a particular kind of journey. I want to warn you that reading *A Quest for More* will at times feel like driving from Kansas to the Pacific coast. It's a great journey, but you no more than get settled in for the trip and you hit the Rocky Mountains. It's easy to get discouraged as you're climbing peak after peak!

What is that mountainous passage that I am talking about? Well, most of the early chapters of this book expose the many, many ways we all tend to forsake the big kingdom for the little kingdom. This part of your journey through the book will be painful at times. You will feel as if you have successfully scaled one peak only to have another in front of you. But don't give up! Once you have the bitter peaks of humble self-examination behind you and have accepted that you have a problem, the sights and sounds of God's solution that are at the end of the journey will look all the more beautiful to you.

As you begin this little journey, remember: It is a sweet thing that we serve a dissatisfied God who has destinations in mind for us that we would never choose for ourselves. It really is a good thing that he will not be satisfied until he has gotten us exactly where he created us and re-created us to be. Most of us would have been satisfied to stay at home, and many of us would have quit the journey long before it was completed. But our heavenly Father won't give up until each one of his children has completed the journey.

So, journey with me, and be aware that there are mountains up ahead. But don't be discouraged. The ocean will soon be in view, and the ardor of the mountains will make your arrival at the destination all the sweeter.

WOULD YOU LIKE YOUR LIFE TO MAKE
A DIFFERENCE?

CHAPTER ONE

A QUEST FOR MORE

*tran·scen·dence: the state of being beyond and
outside of the ordinary range of human experience*

THE BOTTOM LINE: YOU WERE CREATED TO
BE PART OF SOMETHING BIG.

Have you ever wanted to invest yourself in something worthwhile? Have you ever wondered why your life seems to lack meaning or purpose? Have you ever been disappointed when a position, achievement, possession, or relationship failed to fulfill you? Have you ever dreamed that somehow, some way you would be part of something truly great? If so, this book is for you. This book is about having a life that counts for something. It is about living to make a difference.

Now I know that there are many books written about success, achievement, and influence, but this book is different. I want to take you on a journey—a journey through the greatest story ever told, found in the greatest book ever written, the Bible. It is here and here alone that you will begin to discover not only who you are, but what you were meant to be. God has placed you just where he wants you—to be part of something big, right where you are. Yes, you were made to make a difference, so start this journey of discovery with me.

BEAUTY QUEENS AND WORLD PEACE

It is a classic scene in western culture. She stands before the microphone, beautiful and poised, a finalist in the Miss America contest. The host asks her what she would like to accomplish during her reign and she says, "I would like to create world peace, solve world hunger, and liberate all the caged parakeets in the entire world." We've all heard it a hundred times. It has been the fodder for many late-night, stand-up comedy routines. Yet, for all of our cynical smiles and sarcastic comments in the face of the contestant's grandiosity, there is something deeply and uniquely human about what she has said. There is woven inside each of us a desire for something more—a craving to be part of something bigger, greater, and more profound than our relatively meaningless day-by-day existence. Maybe that's why a human being would ever want to climb Everest, traverse the oceans in an all-too-small sailboat, or attempt any feat not yet accomplished by a fellow human. Perhaps that's why we get hooked on politics, sports, or a myriad of causes that give us something to fight for.

We simply weren't constructed to live only for ourselves. We were placed on earth to be part of something bigger than the narrow borders of our own survival and our own little definition of happiness. The desire resides in each of us, and it is called *transcendence.* To transcend is to be part of something greater. We were created to be part of something so big, so glorious, so far beyond the ordinary that it would totally change the way we approach every ordinary thing in our lives. And in all of sin's blindness, brokenness, and rebellion, that desire to transcend has now been crushed.

Being a fan in the stands with 65,000 other fans at the Super Bowl with everyone screaming at the top of their lungs as the kicker launches that last-second field goal gives us a feeling of transcendence. You hear it in the voice of the fan who says, "It's our year! Our time has come! We're going to win this one!" He sounds like he is a paid member of the team, yet he is not. The "we" language is transcendence. He has become part of something greater than his mundane workaday world. His connection to his local team has helped him, if just for a moment, to transcend the small boundaries of his average-guy world. The local worker in the presidential campaign has much the same experience. No, he will probably never meet the candidate face to face; and yes, he is only running folding machines and stuffing boxes full of literature. But he is part of something transcendent. He has been told that this campaign could forever change the face of American politics. His campaign involvement has helped him escape the little world of his small college life to become an integral part of something bigger. If only for a moment, he has transcended.

The mountain climber facing the dizzying heights, the unforgiving inclines, and the biting wind has touched a bit of transcendence. He is about to join a small society of people who have escaped the everyday concerns and demands of life to accomplish something great. He stands on that oxygen-poor summit and he has transcended if for just one day. The mountain isn't the only summit he has ascended.

The marcher in the protest, the career soldier in the combat unit, and the little boy who is pretending he is the king of the world experience the same rush. It is that feeling of being part of something significant, of your place and your part mattering. For a moment your life seems bigger than your life. This bigger thing yanks you out of bed in the morning, and sometimes the excitement of it all makes it hard to sleep. It makes all of the little things that you have to do every day seem more satisfying and more important because they are now connected to something more than self-survival. You have experienced a bit of transcendence.

This desire for transcendence is in all of us because God placed it there. He constructed us to live for more than ourselves. He designed us to want meaning, purpose, and consequence. We were not wired to be fully satisfied with self-survival and self-pleasure. God purposed that the borders of our vision would be much, much larger than the boundaries of our lives. We were meant to see more than our physical eyes can see, and it is that greater vision that was meant to engage, excite, connect, and satisfy us.

Maybe the beauty contestant isn't being so silly after all. Maybe in that moment she has gotten something right. Perhaps her desire for transcendence is a more beautiful part of her humanity than her physical beauty will ever be.

AND NOW FOR THE BEGINNING

There is definitely an "above and more" positioning of human beings in the creation accounts of Genesis 1 and 2. Adam and Eve were not the highest of the animals. The whole account presents them as being unique, different, and above the rest of the things that God made. It is just as clear, too, that these two people were made for more than their own existence. They weren't placed in the garden for self-survival and self-satisfaction. They were immediately given a vision and commission that would take them far beyond the borders of their own needs and concerns. Transcendence was a part of their humanity. They were given amazing capacities to do what no other creature could do. Anything less would be a subhuman existence.

Think about what this means for all of us who are the sons and daughters of Adam and Eve. You and I were created for more than filling up our schedules with the self-satisfying pursuits of personal pleasure. We were meant to do more than make sure that all of our needs are fulfilled and all our desires are satisfied. We were never meant to be self-focused little kings ruling miniscule little kingdoms with a population of one. Sure, it's right for you to care about your health, your job, your house, your investments, your family, and your friends. It would be irresponsible to act as if none of those things mattered. Yet it is a functional human tragedy to live *only* for those things. It is a fundamental denial of your humanity to narrow the size of your life to the size of your own existence, because you were created to be an "above and more" being. You were made to be transcendent.

Jim sat before me, his slumped body a testament to the depression that gripped him. He said he had awakened a few months earlier and realized that there was no one who cared if he woke up that morning. No one cared if he was healthy or sick. No one cared if he was happy or sad. He said, "I get up in the morning and put on great looking clothes, leave my beautiful, modern condominium, get in my luxury car and drive to my high-paying job, only to go back to my beautiful condominium at the end of the day to start it all over again. I could die today and no one would even notice. I have it all; why can't I be happy?" Jim *did* have it all, yet in getting it all he had denied his own humanity. In his quest for everything, Jim had missed the one thing that separated him from everything else that God made. Jim had constructed his own kingdom, indulged his every dream, and met his every need. He had ruled his kingdom with discipline and success, but he discovered that it was an empty kingdom, and he was an empty king. It was not that Jim had attempted too much. The tragedy was that he had settled for way too little, and that is exactly what he got.

How about you? What is the big vision that you're working toward? What is the big dream you are investing in? What is your definition of the "good life"? When will you know that you have been successful? If you had it all, what would "all" look like? I am afraid there are many people of faith who attend church each week, give regularly to God's work, know their Bible pretty well, and don't live overtly evil lives; but they have settled for "below and less" when they were created for "above and more."

The mistake that they have made is that they have shrunk their Christianity to the size of their own lives. They have taken God's grace and wisdom as an invitation to a better marriage, a better relationship with their children, a better extended family life, better success at work, etc. And there is a way that God's grace *does* invite me to all of these things. But here is the point of this little book: God invites you to *so much more!* God's grace invites you to be part of something that is far greater than your boldest and most expansive dream. His grace cuts a hole in your self-built prison and invites you to step into something so huge, so significant that only one word in the Bible can adequately capture it. That word is ***glory***.

HARDWIRED FOR GLORY

Admit it. You're a glory junkie. That's why you like the 360°, between-the-legs, slam dunk, or that amazing hand-beaded formal gown, or the seven-layer triple-chocolate mousse cake. It's why you're attracted to the hugeness of the mountain range or the multihued splendor of the sunset. You were hardwired by your Creator for a glory orientation. It is inescapable. It's in your genes. The groundhogs don't compete for who has made the most glorious underground den. Or, as my brother Tedd says, the penguins don't score one another as they dive off the ice into the frigid sea. There is no penguin announcer who says, "That was a 9.3, had high technical merit, but lacked artistic creativity." But we're different. We'll flock to a museum to see the Salvador Dali masterworks. We'll wait in a ninety-minute line for a ride on the ultimate roller coaster. We'll dream for days about the glory of the upcoming Thanksgiving feast. And we'll work like crazy to achieve one glory moment in some area of our lives. We were simply made for glory, but not just the shadow glories of the created world. We were made for the one glory that is transcendent—the *glory of God*. When you grasp this, your life begins to make a difference.

THE GLORY THAT TRANSCENDS

Now, let me talk for a minute about purpose. There is a way in which this book is about living with purpose. Yet it is about so much more than that. There are many people who have lived lives of purpose that didn't really make much of a difference. Every person's life is purposeful because every human being lives in pursuit of something. So, it is not enough to determine to have purpose. Let me state it this way: It is a good thing to have purpose, but if your purpose isn't tied to glory, you have still denied your humanity.

Let's consider the glory-focus of Genesis 1 and 2. There are four transcendent glories that were created to be the life-shaping focus of every human being. The first is the glory for which every human is to live, and the following three are glories that flow from the first. Each of these calls us out of the tight confines of a self-oriented existence to something fundamentally above and beyond. We will introduce them here and expand on each throughout the book.

God glory. We were made to be more connected to what is above us than to what is below us. To put it another way, our lives were designed to be shaped more by our attachment to the Creator than by the creation. We were made to experience, to be part of, to be consumed by, and to live in pursuit of the one glory that is truly glorious—the glory of God. A ravenous and not easily satisfied pursuit of this glory is meant to be the compass of our living. In Genesis 1, God comes on scene the minute Adam and Eve take their first breath. He is there to command their allegiance. He is there to be the central focus of everything they ever think, desire, say, and do—and when he is, their lives have transcendent meaning and purpose. Here's what this means. The transcendent glory that every human being quests for, whether he knows it or not, is not a thing; it is a person, and his name is *God*. People are transcendent because people were made for him. It is only in communion with him and in submitting all other forms of glory to his glory that I will ever find the "above and more" that my heart seeks. God's immediate presence in the lives of Adam and Eve is a call to the ultimate in transcendence. They are to live for the One who *is* glory. And they must never shrink the size of their glory focus to the narrow glories of their own little lives.

Stewardship glory. It is amazing as you read the story of creation to see that God carefully constructed his world and then placed it in the hands of people. God gave Adam and Eve the responsibility for being good and faithful stewards of everything he had made. In effect, they were designed to be God's "resident managers." Their vision of personal purpose was meant to be as wide as the universe that God had created. They were constructed to do more than take care of themselves; they were called to care for the wide variety of amazing things God had purposefully crafted to be reflectors of his glory. The transcendence of human beings is expressed as people reflect God's glory by their rulership and stewardship over the surrounding created world. This call to manage the created order was a divine call to transcendence. It was a call for Adam and Eve to never shrink the size of their care to care for themselves.

Community glory. You and I were made for relationships. Adam wasn't meant to live alone. Adam wasn't meant to be Adam's best friend. The community that Adam and Eve were meant to live in with one another was designed to be the beginning of a huge web of interdependent human relationships that would define much of the focus and energy of peoples' lives. Human beings' lives were meant to transcend the narrow glories of independence, autonomy, and self-sufficiency. We were created to have lives shaped by a constant pursuit of the glory of humble, dependent community. We were made to need one another, and this community was meant to exist in a variety of forms, including neighbor, family, friend, church, city, state, nation, brother, sister, parent, and spouse. This web of ongoing relationships daily calls us out of our insulation and isolation to experience a community glory that selfish, personal focus can never deliver.

God makes Adam and Eve and immediately calls them to the transcendent glory of a world-reaching, generation-spanning, and history-encompassing community. This commitment to community was meant to be a major shaping focus of their day-by-day living. This act of God to immediately tie Adam and Eve into community with one another was a call to transcendence. It was a call to never shrink the size of their community to a functional community of one.

Truth glory. Immediately upon creating Adam and Eve, God did something that he had not done with anything else he made. He spoke to them. This mundane moment was a moment of transcendence! The Lord, King, and Creator of the universe was speaking the secrets of his divine wisdom into the ears of the people he had made. In this act God was calling Adam and Eve to transcend the boundaries of their own thoughts, interpretations, and experiences. They were to form their lives by the origin-to-destiny perspective that only the Creator could have. God had hardwired Adam and Eve with the communicative abilities that they would need in order to receive his revelation, because the glorious truths that God would progressively unfold to them were meant to shape everything they thought, desired, decided, and did. Their lives were set apart from all of the rest of creation because God had opened his truth glory to them and them alone. By themselves they never could have discovered the things he told them. These treasures of wisdom would only be known by Adam and Eve because God decided to reveal them. God's words contained knowledge of him, the meaning and purpose of life, a moral structure for living, the nature of human identity, a fundamental human job description, a call to human community, and a call to divine worship. Never were Adam and Eve built to exist on conclusions drawn from their experience, or concepts resulting from autonomous interpretations. Every thought was meant to be shaped by the truth glory that he would patiently and progressively impart to them. God's seemingly mundane act of communication in the garden was in fact a call to transcendence. It was a call to an "above and more" way of living. It was a call to Adam and Eve to never shrink the size of their thought down to the size of their thoughts.

BUT WAIT A MINUTE! WHAT ABOUT TUESDAY?

Maybe as you've been reading, you've been thinking, "Okay, Paul, what you have been talking about is all very interesting, but I'm living real life here! For example, on Tuesday I have to go to school with my teenage son to talk about his rapidly failing grades. In the afternoon I have to meet with a friend to deal with a misunderstanding between us, and in the evening I have to talk with my husband about our finances. I'm facing a whole lot of real-life issues that I don't really want to face, and I don't think I have time for transcendence!"

But, hang in here with me. This *is* the point of this book. In a fallen world there is a powerful pressure to constrict your life to the shape and size of your life. There is a compelling tendency to forget who you are and what you were made for. There is a tendency to be shortsighted, myopic, and easily distracted. There is a tendency to settle for less when you have been created for more. There is something expansive, glorious, and eternal that is meant to give direction to everything you do. And when you lose sight of it, you have effectively denied your own humanity.

You see, all of those things you will do on Tuesday are necessary and important. This book is not a call to forget them and do something else. No, it is about a whole new way of approaching these things. It is about a way of living where God has placed me that embraces the transcendent glories for which I was created. It is about living for a greater kingdom than the kingdom of my life, my family, and my job. And where do I live for this greater kingdom? In my life, in my family, and in my job! This book was not written to call to you to stop doing everything you have been doing or to start doing a bunch of new things. Rather, it is a call to do what God has called you to do with a vision that is as broad and deep as the glory of God.

This book is a call to plan large and live big. It is an encouragement to let God glory, community glory, stewardship glory, and truth glory alter the way you deal with everything that is on your plate. It is an encouragement to remember and affirm that your humanity only really lives when it is connected to the transcendent glory that can only be found in God.

Are you not sure what all of this means? Are you unsure of what it would practically look like? Do you want to live a life that really counts for something and that makes a difference? Take time to read on.

THE FINAL QUESTION: WHAT IS THE BIG THING THAT YOU ARE LIVING FOR RIGHT NOW?

HAVE YOU BEEN WILLING TO
SETTLE FOR LESS?

CHAPTER TWO

MORE OR LESS?

pre·tense: a false appearance or action intended to deceive

THE BOTTOM LINE: SIN CAUSES US TO TALK ABOUT MORE, BUT TO SETTLE FOR LESS.

It was one of those moments, small and unimportant in one way, but a sign of something very significant when looked at from another perspective. We were on our way somewhere. Because of my eye problems, Luella often drives in the evening. As she headed off toward our location, I said, "Don't you want to turn there?"—just when we passed the street where I would've turned.

She replied, "That way will take too long."

"The shortest distance between two points is a straight line," I reminded her.

"That's exactly why I didn't turn!"

"But you're taking us way out of the way," I insisted.

"Why don't you just relax and let me drive?"

"Because I don't trust your sense of direction!"

Luella offered, "Let's make a deal. When you're driving, you get to decide the route, and when I'm driving I'll decide the route."

"But what if you're going the wrong way?"

"It's not a matter of right and wrong; it's simply a matter of preference."

And I thought (without saying it), *But my preference is right!* Instead I said, "I wish we were in a helicopter so I could show you the whole route. Then you would understand what I'm trying to tell you."

Luella replied, "I don't think a helicopter is what you need right now!"

It was a moment of minor irritation, never exploding into full-blown anger, yet a moment that is worth unpacking. What this conversation reveals is how hard it is for fallen human beings to keep focused on what is really important. In a heated moment all of us are quite capable of treating a minor detail of life as if it were a major thing. We are all capable of fighting for what has little value while forgetting things of transcendent value.

In a flash of irritation, a mom will treat the condition of her son's bedroom as being more valuable than the community she is to have with her son, which is so essential to what God wants to do for this boy through her. After months of frustration, a believer will get into a heated argument over garden boundaries with his neighbor, forgetting how much more important it is to be salt and light in the man's life than how many flowers were planted over the property line. For a moment, a man will get more of a sense of well-being from the look and smell of his brand-new car than he does from the condition of his heart. For a season, the affection and appreciation of another human being will become more functionally important to us than the gracious, forgiving, and adopting love of our heavenly Father. For a moment, a succulent steak becomes more important to us than a soul that has been satisfied by the Living Bread. In the flash of one look, the beauty and shape of a woman's body can become more important than long-term marital community and a heart that is pure. And in a car on a given night, being right in the eyes of your spouse can become more important than living right before your Lord.

It is so hard for us to get glory right. It is so hard for us to see through all the near "glories" of creation to see the transcendent glory of God. It is so difficult for us to remember and be motivated by what is truly important. It is so tempting to be committed to our little kingdoms that the transcendent kingdom of God is of little functional influence. We are in fact in a great war, the daily melodrama of the heart. This is exactly what was happening to me that night in the car. It happens to each of us every day. We again and again deny our humanity as we settle for something less than the transcendent glories for which we were created. It is so hard for us to make the truly important things functionally important to us. And it didn't take long for Adam and Eve to fall into this trouble as well.

TROUBLE IN THE GARDEN

Have you ever thought about what exactly the Serpent offered Eve in that fateful conversation in the garden? What he offered Eve was "more." What he offered Eve was transcendence, but it had a fatal flaw. It wasn't connected to God! Here was an offer of an "above and beyond" glory, but it was a replacement for the transcendent glory that can only be found in God. Notice the thundering implication of these five simple words, "You will be like God." The Serpent was saying, *You know, Eve, there is a greater, more satisfying glory than anything you have yet experienced. Your life can be much, much more than it has already been. Why, Eve, you can have it all. If you would just be willing to step outside of God's narrow boundaries, you wouldn't need to be connected to him, because you would be like him.*

These manipulative words of the enemy appear to offer greater transcendence but are really shrinking it dramatically. The glory that the Serpent holds out is no glory at all. Let me state it this way: When I opt for a me-centered "more," what I actually get is always much, much less. Essentially Satan is saying, *Eve, you can live for a greater and more satisfying kingdom than the kingdom of God. If you do this one thing, you can have a kingdom where you are central and where you rule unchallenged.* It is the same evil sales pitch that Satan offered to Christ at the beginning of his ministry on earth. (See Matthew 4:8–11.) Here we have recorded the very first time in human history when a person was willing to restrict her living to the size of her life. We have been paying the price ever since.

USED CAR SALES

I like to listen to used-car salesmen. Not all of them are like what I am about to describe, but I think the word craft they employ is instructive. Deceptive sales craft is all about embellishment of the positive, shrinking the negative, and a careful sprinkling of pretenses (plausible lies). You walk up to what is designed to be a mode of transportation, and the salesman immediately says to you, "This baby has the finest sound system you'll ever find in a car. And sit in those seats. They're capable of over fifty different positions." Now that he has so overstated a couple of the car's positives so that you are not thinking about the engine and transmission, he seeks to shrink the negatives in your thinking. He says, "It's a great car for driving around the city." This actually means it is very small and doesn't have much pick-up. He adds, "It is a perfect car for a young family." He actually means that the back seat is so small that no normal-sized human being could ever sit there comfortably. Then he ends with plausible lies. He says, "We will have no trouble making it affordable for you." This probably means, "You cannot afford this car, but we can manipulate the finances in such a way as to make you think you can."

Such is the craft of the enemy. It is all about embellishment, negation, and plausible lies. It is the craft of temptation. It is the craft of pseudo-glory and false transcendence. It is a wicked craft, but it gets us again and again.

You see, the enemy of our souls knows that we were created for transcendence. He knows that we were created to be constantly connected to something more glorious than the small glories of our own survival and pleasure. He knows that we all hunger for more, so his craft is to present us with less in a way that makes it appear to be more. The "you can be like God" offer in the garden was not an honest invitation to more; it was a deceitful trick that would only lead to less. It was not an invitation to be more gloriously human, but a pitch to get Adam and Eve to deny the fundamental basis of their true humanity. Yet their humanity was connected to the glory of God, and to disobey him would never ever lead to greater glory.

IT'S ALWAYS THE SAME OLD SET OF TRICKS

Every day, in many ways, we give in to the same old set of tricks. We forget the transcendence for which we were made and we look at much lesser things as if they were more. The cost to us is just as huge as it was to Adam and Eve. Naked, guilty, and embarrassed, they hid from their God in the bushes of the garden.

A man will forget that, as a father, he has been welcomed to the transcendent glory of being part of God's work of forming human souls. Instead he will buy into the replacement glory of career success. More and more, his life will be eaten up and defined by his work. Less and less will his sense of purpose have to do with the formative community that only he can offer his children. Sadly, his children cease to be one of the joyful focuses of his living and become an obligation in an already-too-busy schedule. Less and less do his children know him, respect him, trust him, or feel his love.

A young person will forget the transcendent glory of an identity that is rooted in the presence, power, and grace of the Redeemer. Instead she will live for the pseudo-glory of the approval of peers. She'll pick up on and parrot her friends' vocabulary, she'll take on their sense of style, she'll laugh obviously at their jokes, and she'll even participate in activities that prick her conscience—all because she has convinced herself that she "needs" their approval. There will be moments when she will feel transcendent. She will feel as if her life has real meaning and purpose because she is connected to something bigger than herself. The sad fact is that she has opted for less. The community of her peers has actually become a replacement community for the transcendent glory of loving, worshipful, daily community with the Lord. And the things that she hopes she will find in the acceptance of her peers, no human being is ever able to give to her. She will only ever find it in the accepting grace of God.

It may be that we settle for less in moments that are much less consequential than these. Being right can replace being kind, being served can replace the joy of serving, power can trump character, possessions can become more attractive than spiritual blessings, and a moment of independence can become more compelling than long-term interdependent community. Even getting the last cookie can become more important than the love we are meant to mutually share.

Here it is. When the enemy somehow tricks you into squeezing the size of your life to the size of your personal dreams, wants, and needs, he has got you right where he wants you. He has won a victory every time he successfully tempts you to exchange the God-centered more for which you were created, replacing it with one of the endless catalog of me-centered "mores" that dangle before us in this fallen world. His lie is this: "Transcendence is really found when you live at the center of your world." Or, "Ultimate joy and satisfaction is found when you live for you."

Now you may be saying, "Come on, Paul, I'm biblically smart enough to know that that isn't true!" You probably do, but the struggle I am describing very often takes place inside the borders of good theology and regular participation in the scheduled programs of the church. It is possible, and maybe even quite regular, to participate in these things and still be settling, in the little moments of our daily existence, for much, much less than the transcendence for which we were created. Things as mundane as wardrobe, menu, schedule, workload, location, traffic, weather, being right, getting affirmed, money, housing, employment, gardens, family rooms, sex, leisure, who's in the bathroom first, who did what with my newspaper, who ate the last of the cereal, etc.—all of which are important in some way—rise to a spiritually dangerous level of importance in the heat of the moment. These are the moments we live in every day. The normal day is a 24-hour collection of little moments. Day after day, week after week, and year after year, these little moments set the character of a person's life.

When little things become the big thing for which I consistently fight, I have forsaken transcendence for the temporary shadow glories of creation. The temporary satisfaction and pleasure that I get will not last. These things are like spiritual crack; they will give me a quick emotional or spiritual rush, while leaving me unfilled and hungering for the next rush.

This has always been the struggle of God's people. Think of Israel in the wilderness. What causes them to actually consider going back to Egypt? Menu! (See Numbers 11.) They were tired of this quasi-tasteless substance called manna. Think about it for a moment. The flavor of a God-provided food rose to such a level of importance that they were actually able to look at Egypt as a place with a better menu, rather than the place of slavery and death that it actually was.

Think about what initiated the heinous idolatry of Israel at the base of Mt Sinai. Was it not a matter of schedule? (See Exodus 32:1.) Moses had been too long on the mountain. The children of Israel were impatient, so they said, "Moses has been gone so long we don't know what's happened to him, so let's make gods who will go before us." Is schedule important? Is there legitimacy to wondering what has happened to your leader if he has been absent for awhile? Of course there is! But this legitimate concern becomes fundamentally more important than it ever should be, and when it does, it completely distorts the perspective of the people and sets them up for spiritual danger.

Or consider the disciples in the upper room in the final hours before Christ's capture. He sits with them as Messiah, Priest, and Lamb. He, in this moment and in the sacrificial moments to come, is instituting the New Covenant. There could be no more significant moment of redemptive importance. Yet, Luke tells us that in the middle of this moment of high and holy drama, the disciples are arguing about who of them is greatest! (See Luke 22:24–30.) Are position, power, and affirmation of no consequence whatsoever? Of course not! But when they rise to the level of overwhelming the crashing significance of being welcomed into the kingdom of God, of eating at the table with the Lord of the universe, and of sitting on thrones built by him, then something has gone drastically wrong. In this moment the disciples are forsaking the transcendent glories of the kingdom of God for the pseudo-glory of personal power and position.

Take a moment to consider Peter in Galatia, who has let his fear of a certain set of Jews rise to a level of greater importance than the transcendent freedom glories of the gospel for which he had been chosen to be a spokesman. (See Galatians 2:11–14.) Something as normal as a concern over what others think of me, or what will happen to me if others oppose me, rises to a level of such immediate importance that my actions are more shaped by that concern than they are about the huge and transcendent glories of the life-altering grace of the gospel.

So, how are you doing with transcendence? What is the "more" for which you are questing? Examine the last few weeks. What is rising to a level of decision-making, behavior-shaping importance in your life? Inside your correct theology and your faithful participation in the gatherings and ministries of the body of Christ, is your life a picture of the transcendence atrophy? Have you exchanged "more" for "less"? While affirming what is right, have you functionally settled for what is really a subtle, but significant, rejection of the true humanity for which you were created? True humanity is always connected to glory, and true glory can only be found in the One who is glory, the Lord.

In how many mundane ways each week are you tempted to compress the size of your living to the concerns of your life? You can even shrink the glory-call and the glory-promises of the gospel down to excitement with a little bit better marriage, slightly more responsive children, and some principles that will help you be more successful at your job. Does God offer me these things? Sure he does! But he calls me to so much more. He calls me to find personal glory in his glory, and in so doing, to be committed to community, stewardship, and truth glory as well.

If Genesis 1 is a welcome to transcendence, then Genesis 3 is about the tragedy of the shrinking of transcendence. Adam and Eve were created so that their lives would reach as wide as the kingdom and glory of God. In that one disastrous moment they did not expand their boundaries; they dramatically narrowed them. The vertical "more" for which transcendent human beings were created was replaced by a horizontal "more" that was never to be a human being's life motivation. In that one tragic moment, Adam and Eve migrated to the center of their world, the one place where glory-wired human beings must never live. They did not just opt for independence; they opted for God's position, and in doing so they forsook any chance of a personal participation in the transcendent glory of a relationship with God.

This is why God sent his Redeemer Son to earth. He came to rescue us from ourselves and return to us participation in his transcendence. In his adoption we are restored to the *God glory* which is to be central to everything we do. In his church we are restored to the *community glory* in which we were built to participate. In freeing us from idolatry, rather than being ruled by the creation, we are restored to the *stewardship glory* over creation to which we were called. In the ministry of his indwelling Spirit, through Scripture, we are restored to the *truth glory* that was meant to be the interpretive lens of every human being since Adam took his first breath. His is a gorgeous work of rescue!

Yet, learning to live with the transcendent glories of the created and re-created children of God is a process, not an event. You and I are still in the middle of the process. Sometimes we get it, but often we forget. Sometimes we do act with faith, hope, and courage. Sometimes we really do hold out for "more" and refuse to be manipulated into settling for "less." Sometimes we will not settle for any condition less than being truly human. But sometimes we take the bait and go after less as if it were more. Sometimes, even though grace has expanded our borders until they touch glory, we still reduce the borders of our living to the boundaries of our lives.

If you will stop for a moment and look at yourself, you will recognize evidences of the struggle. The evidences are in your family and friendships. They are there at work and in times of leisure. They are visible in your relationship to your position, possessions, and power. Yes, they are even there in your participation in the body of Christ. So, this book is offered as help in the struggle. It is meant to help you more clearly grasp what it means to live for more. It is meant as a welcome to a life that really makes a difference. You and I were wired for transcendent glory. The big question of life is: What glory will you live for each and every day?

THE FINAL QUESTION: WHAT IS THE "LESS" THAT TENDS TO CAPTURE YOUR ATTENTION?

HAVE YOU EVER
WANTED TO BE . . . GOD?

CHAPTER THREE

A TOTAL DISASTER

au·ton·o·my: the quality or state of being independent, free, and self-directed

THE BOTTOM LINE: SINCE SIN HAS DAMAGED EVERYTHING, GOD CALLS US TO BE CONCERNED ABOUT EVERYTHING.

It was always a moment of panic for us. We would hear her feet on the steps, and we knew what her mission was. She was coming up to inspect the neatness and cleanliness of our bedroom. We would immediately go into rapid-bedroom-restoration mode, but it was always to no avail. There was no way we could ever get it right before her feet touched the last step. The mess was too great and the time too little. She would always hit that last step just as my brother Mark and I were stuffing huge piles of personal belongings under our bed, vainly hoping that this time Mom would be fooled. But she never was. In her anger at the sorry condition of our room and her irritation at our stuff-it-under-the-bed game, she would say the words we hated to hear, "This room is a total disaster!" And we knew that this meant we wouldn't be leaving it until it had been fully restored to its rightful condition.

When Adam and Eve forsook God-centered transcendence for the false-hope, me-centered transcendence that the Serpent offered, the result really was a total disaster. You and I still experience the effects of that disaster every day of our lives. What happened in the garden is truly the central catastrophe of human history. It is almost impossible to overstate the hugeness of its significance. Here is how big this disaster was (and is). When Adam and Eve fell, the entire cosmos fell with them! There is no place to run. There is no refuge in which to hide. There is no situation untouched by its power, no location unharmed by its destruction. In a flash of disobedience and stolen glory, sin wrecked the cosmos. It was a total disaster.

A THING OF STUNNING BEAUTY

God's creative artistry, shown in the world he made and everything he placed in it, was a thing of gorgeous and stunning beauty. The hills were awash in multihued flowers, with no weevil to consume their leaves and no mites to infect their blossoms. The soil was packed with life-giving nutrients, and there were no thorns, thistles, or weeds to be found. Trees were laden with the lushest, sweetest, most succulent fruit. There were no plagues or pollutants. Nature grew, bloomed, and produced without struggle or toil. There was untainted natural beauty as far as the eye could see. It literally covered the earth.

Animals frolicked, fed, mated, and produced without fear of predators or a fight with disease. The animal kingdom was a place of an amazing variegated beauty, all existing in an atmosphere of peace.

People lived in joyful, unafraid, and unashamed community with one another. There was no stealing, lying, cheating, harsh words, abusive actions, strategies of vengeance, sexual immorality, broken families, or corrupt government. No one struggled with depression, anxiety, issues of identity, paralyzing regret, anger, envy, compulsion, addiction, fear, guilt, aloneness, hopelessness, or doubt. People didn't suffer from injury, disease, or old age. There were no hospital vigils and no viewings of the deceased. No one needed to ask for forgiveness and no one struggled to forgive. There was no marital disappointment and no employment gone bad.

People lived in heartfelt, loving, obedient worship of God. They worshipped the Creator and managed creation; they didn't give in to worshipping creation and trying to manage the Creator. There was no doubt of his goodness, no fear of his anger. There was no overt rebellion or subtle disobedience. They obeyed his words and listened to his wisdom. There were no corrupting idols or competing systems of faith. No one was ever angry at God, and God had no cause for anger with the people he had made. People loved God's glory and in no way lived for their own.

In every way you could think or imagine, the world, as God created it, was a place of unparalleled peace and beauty. It was a sight and surround-sound glory display, reflecting the transcendent glory of the One who had made it out of nothing. His creative majesty was on untainted and uninterrupted display: the piercing red of the rose, the fluorescent scales of the fish, the sweet song of the bird, the gray grandeur of the rock, the earth-shaking roar of the lion, the endless gurgling of the stream, and the lacey delicacy of the leaf. Each part pointed to him. Each thing existed as a hymn to his glory.

HOW DO YOU MEASURE A CATASTROPHE?

How do you wrap words around the worse thing that ever happened? Maybe the apostle Paul did it best with this powerful statement in Romans 8:21:

"The whole creation groans." Lilies now fought with weeds that would choke out their lives. Pollutants floated as shadows in the sky and unseen toxins in the stream. Fruit and flower were blighted with disease. Pain, suffering, toil, disease, and death became the regular experience of everything in the creation. What was once very easy was easy no longer. What was simple became terribly complicated. Everything that was once free now was only obtained at great cost. What seemed once unthinkably wrong and out of character for the world that God had made now became a daily experience. Words like falsehood, enemy, danger, sin, destruction, war, murder, sickness, fear, and hatred became regular parts of the fallen-world vocabulary.

For the first time, the harmony between people was broken. Shame, fear, guilt, blame, greed, envy, conflict, and hurt made relationships a minefield they were never intended to be. People looked at other people as obstacles to getting what they wanted or as dangers to be avoided. Even families were unable to coexist in any kind of lasting and peaceful union. Violence became a common response to problems that had never before existed. Conflict existed in the human community as an experience more regular than peace. Marriage became a battle for control, and children's rebellion became a more natural response than willing submission. Things became more valuable than people, and they willingly competed with others in order to acquire more. The human community was more divided by love for self than united by love of neighbor. The words of people, meant to express truth and love, became weapons of anger and instruments of deceit. In an instant, the sweet music of human harmony had become the mournful dirge of human war.

THE SADDEST THING ON EARTH

Yet, with all of the havoc that sin wreaked on the physical world and on the human community, there was another horrible result. It was something so unthinkable, so horrific, so hard to grasp, that it easily stands as the saddest thing that has ever happened on earth. This tragedy is portrayed in a seemingly mundane conversation captured in Genesis 3:8–10.

> Then the man and his wife heard the sound of the LORD God as he was walking in the garden in the cool of the day, and they hid from the LORD God among the trees of the garden. But the LORD God called to the man, "Where are you?"
>
> He answered, "I heard the sound of you in the garden, and I was afraid because I was naked; so I hid."

What a sad, sad moment! Here is a man, created to have the boundaries of his life reach to the furthest boundaries of the glory of God. Here is one who was created to get his identity, meaning, and purpose from an intimate relationship with God. Here is a person whose every word, thought, desire, and deed were meant to be shaped by a heartfelt submission to and worship of his Creator. What do we find him doing? He hides in fear when the One who is meant to *be* his life comes near!

The sadness of this scene penetrates far deeper than formal religion and spirituality. It is about a crushing loss of transcendence, meaning, and purpose! To hide from his Creator is to hide from his true identity. He has done the one thing that he never, ever was supposed to do. In a moment of conscious rebellion, he has treated his life as being no bigger than his life. As a result, his response to God's presence is not delight and love, but guilt and fear. He knows what he has done. He has forsaken the transcendent glory for which he was created and chosen a replacement glory: to take for himself the glory that only God was to have. He has compressed the borders of his life to his own wants, needs, and desires. It is the small world of autonomy, too small for real life to ever exist there. This self-centered world lacks the oxygen of relationship with God. It is not a place of life. It is a place of death.

How sad! Created for more, Adam and Eve chose less instead. Forgetting who they were, they attempted to find life outside of God, but what they found instead was death.

AUTONOMY AND TRANSCENDENCE

What did the Serpent hold out to Adam and Eve that was attractive enough for them to consider stepping away from the one central thing for which they were made? He offered them an *independent* glory. If they would just step out on their own, they could be transcendent beings like God. The word for this is *autonomy*. Here was the lie (and one that is still being whispered in the ears of people every day): "The key to true transcendence *is* autonomy." But it was a wicked and cruel lie. The quest for autonomy will always crush transcendence. Rather than the huge glories of living for the glory of God, I end up with little shadow glories filling the dim cubicle of my own glory. As 2 Corinthians 5:15 makes clear, human beings were never meant to "live for themselves." So, when Jesus touches me with his rescuing grace, he is freeing me from my bondage to me!

Since that horrible moment in the garden, every human being has tended to confuse autonomy with transcendence. The inertia of sin is always away from the Creator and toward ourselves. And let it be known that this is not only the struggle of the unbeliever; it is the struggle of the believer as well. As long as sin still dwells in our hearts, autonomy will war with transcendence. We are quite able to shrink the transcendent promises, glories, and hopes of the gospel to the size of our own lives, forgetting that, by God's grace, we have been rescued from our self-constructed cubicle and welcomed to the vast expansiveness of the kingdom of God. One day the war between independence and transcendence will end, and we will live in glory, with glory, forever.

UNTIL THEN

I once had a friend who hired a contractor to build a new house for his family. Their budget was very limited, so they could only afford to have the contractor get them under a roof and do all the rough carpentry work. They had to complete all the interior finish work after they had already moved into their "new" home. I can remember him saying to me, "We are very thankful for our new house, but we have to keep reminding ourselves that the job isn't done yet, and we have to stay focused and working until it is." In the same way, each of us should be deeply grateful for our inclusion in God's family of grace. We should be very excited about the way that grace has radically changed our lives. But we must also be aware that God has not yet completed his work in us. Yes, every day in some way you and I demonstrate that there is more work to be done. Maybe it is a word of irritation. Perhaps it is shown in a moment of selfishness or greed. Maybe it is a refusal to admit wrong or a willingness to shift blame. It may be revealed in a thought of lust or a compromise of biblical conviction. Maybe it is in the all too frequent conflicts in my marriage or with my children. Maybe it is in my unwillingness to accept my job or my financial state. The point is that the evidence is there that the work of God's grace in each of our lives is not done yet.

Because of this there are two things that I must always keep in view. ***The ongoing tendency to treat my life as if it were no bigger than my life.*** We all need to be examining the places where we still tend to "live for ourselves." Maybe this comes out as being more personally excited by the acquisition of a material thing than by growing in my relationship with the Lord. Maybe it comes out as being in conflict with another person because they are in the way of something I am convinced that I need. Maybe it is eating or spending more than I should. Maybe it is exhibited by a stronger desire to "win" a conversation than a desire for loving unity. Maybe it is that my involvement in my local church has been whittled down to a Sunday slot in an already too busy schedule. There is a great temptation in all of us to reduce all that God has taught us and done in us down to the size of the personal concerns of our lives. Yes, it is right to be excited. The work of Christ *will* help you enjoy a better marriage, be a better friend, enjoy better relationships with your children, and do better at work. It *is* true that if you deal with your heart issues you will make progress in all of these areas. But God has called you to a greater circle of concern than your own life. You see, when God enters our lives by his grace, he isn't working to make our kingdom work so much as he is calling us to an excitement with, and dedication to, a much greater kingdom.

Most of us have learned how to celebrate our inclusion in God's great and glorious work, while functionally caring for little that does not directly address us. In doing this we have Christianized our autonomy. Essentially, we are asking God to give his endorsement to our attempt to shrink the transcendent glories of his kingdom to the size of our circle of personal concern. And even though we are trying to live inside of God's boundaries, we have still manufactured a life where self is at the center. It is quite possible for our Christianity to be quite narrow and selfish and to not be aware of the shrinkage.

We must keep in mind that the fall was a total disaster. Again, it is hard to find words that do justice to the unimaginable devastation that sin wreaked on everything that God created. Its effect was total and complete. You may be wondering why it is so important to keep the comprehensive nature of the fall of the world in your mind. This is necessary because it is only when you remember how big the effects of sin are that you will live the way God calls you to live. Here is the logic of living in light of the purposes of God: If sin's devastation is as wide as creation, then the scope of redemption must be just as big. Therefore, we are called to live with the total restoration of creation in view.

What is the kingdom of God all about? What is the new life to which God has called me? What new meaning and purpose is to become the focus of my life as a child of God? What in the world are we Christians supposed to be doing anyway?

God has called us away from our autonomous, self-focused living to live transcendently once again. This means to live with restoration in view in every situation, location, and relationship in which God places me. And what is God's redemptive purpose? It is captured in the second to last chapter in the Bible, when God, seated on the throne says, "I am making everything new!" (Revelation 21:5). It is summarized in Romans 8:18–24, which pictures the whole of creation groaning, waiting for redemption. If the glory of God is reflected in all of creation, if the effects of sin reach to all of creation, and if the goal of redemption is to restore all of creation, then what should you and I care about? EVERYTHING!

Your sadness with sin should be bigger than the fact that it complicates your life. Your sadness should extend as far as sin reaches. Your celebration of God's restoring grace should be bigger than the fact that it brings blessing to your private world. No, your celebration should reach as far as restoration is needed. God's grace really does welcome you to *think big* and *live large*. God invites you to be an active and daily part of the "more" of redemption. His restoring grace gives you reason to extend the boundaries of your concern way beyond the borders of your own life. He calls you out of your little kingdom to give your talents, gifts, resources, and time to the glorious concerns of his big sky kingdom.

As his child, when you get up in the morning you awake to a huge kingdom. It courses back through history and extends to before the foundations of the world were set in place. It extends forward in time to endless eternity. It encompasses every location known and unknown, every situation of every kind, every person and every created thing. The goal of this kingdom is the complete restoration of every last thing that was damaged by the fall. You must no longer live for yourself. Grace has led you through the door to something more and better. Grace calls you to shape your living to the contours of this amazing work of restoration. As the great old Christmas carol proclaims, "He comes to make his blessings known, far as the curse is found." ("Joy to the World")

But this is precisely where our problem takes place. We get so excited about the personal benefits of redemption that we lose sight of redemption's greater goal. Yes, the personal benefits of redemption are amazing, worthy of eternal celebration. But redemption's agenda is not to make our kingdoms successful, but to welcome us to a much bigger, much better kingdom.

Jim Collins makes this stunning observation in his best-selling book on corporate management, *Good to Great.*

> Good is the enemy of great. And that is one of the key reasons why we have so little that becomes great. We don't have great schools, principally because we have good schools. We don't have great government, principally because we have good government. Few people attain great lives, in large part because it is just so easy to settle for a good life.[1]

Collins's observation is so important! Many of you have done just what he is talking about with your walk with the Lord. You have settled into a self-focused enjoyment of the good life. You are enjoying what grace has done to your marriage, your parenting, your friendships, and your work life. It has been all too easy for you to miss the point that you were rescued from what was very bad—not just to be part of something good, but amazingly, to be part of something very great.

You have been chosen to *transcend*—to transcend the boundaries of your own hopes and dreams, to transcend the boundaries of your own plans and purposes, and to transcend the borders of your own family and friends. You have been chosen to transcend the furthest reach of your own definition of glory to be part of a greater glory, the glory of God and his work of making all things new.

Have you settled for living too small? In the midst of the total disaster of sin, have you settled for something good when you have been chosen for something great?

THE FINAL QUESTION: HAVE YOU TREATED THE SIZE OF GOD'S GRACE AS IF IT WERE NO BIGGER THAN THE SIZE OF YOUR PERSONAL CONCERNS?

ARE YOU TRYING TO BUILD
YOUR OWN KINGDOM?

CHAPTER FOUR

WELCOME TO MY LITTLE KINGDOM

king·dom: a realm or sphere in which one thing is dominant

THE BOTTOM LINE: EACH OF OUR LIVES IS SHAPED BY THE WAR BETWEEN THE KINGDOM OF GOD AND THE KINGDOM OF SELF.

It was called Puzzletown, and it was his own little kingdom. From the earliest moments of his life, Ethan, our second son, was our artist and dreamer. He was not only in his own world; he constructed it! And when he discovered Puzzletown, it was like he had finally found everything he had been looking for. Puzzletown was a three-dimensional construction toy that allowed the child to build a little community with houses, shops, and gardens. All of the sudden, he was the lord and maker of his own little world! The little town served his purpose and did according to his will. He would spend hours in "Ethan Kingdom," losing track of time as he enjoyed being creator and in charge.

Ethan is a man now, and Puzzletown is safely stored away in our basement. But I would imagine that Ethan's desire for kingdom building is still there, as it is in you and me as well. You see, we are all kingdom builders. The issue is whose kingdom are we building?

Let me take you back to the garden one more time. In that devious conversation with Eve, the Serpent was selling her a "better" kingdom. In this kingdom she would be the one on the throne. This kingdom would be about her will and her way. What Satan said he was offering Eve was something bigger and better, but what he really offered her was much less and infinitely smaller.

Ever since that fateful day, human life and history has been shaped by kingdoms in conflict. The little kingdom wars with the big kingdom, the kingdom of this world wars with the kingdom of heaven, and the kingdom of man wars with the kingdom of God. This war goes on behind every human intention, decision, thought, word, desire, and deed. Everything everyone ever does is done in pursuit of the success of one of these kingdoms. This war is unceasing and inescapable because it is fought on the turf of each of our hearts. Created for "big kingdom" living, sin twists our allegiance and causes us to be all too dedicated to the little kingdoms of our own making. We get blinded to the transcendent glories of the big kingdom and actually believe that the little shadow glories of our own little kingdom are as good as it gets.

The problem is that most of us don't think in kingdom terms. You know, you just rather thoughtlessly get up in the morning and go to work, or get the kids ready for school, or take the dog for a walk, or read the morning paper. You and I don't live with a ready sense of our intentions or allegiances. And this is precisely how we get ourselves into trouble. Without knowing it, we can reduce the promises of Scripture down to a hope that God's grace will ensure the success of our little kingdoms. Instead, the promises of the Bible are an invitation to active participation in a bigger and better kingdom, the kingdom of God. And where do you pursue the interests of the big kingdom? In exactly the same place where you are tempted to pursue the little kingdom, right where you live and work each day.

TREASURES AND LILIES

What does *little kingdom* living look like? Jesus brilliantly answers this question in Matthew 6.

> Do not store up for yourselves treasures on earth, where moth
> and rust destroy, and where thieves break in and steal. But store
> up for yourselves treasures in heaven, where moth and rust do not
> destroy, and where thieves do not break in and steal. For where
> your treasure is, there your heart will be also.
>
> The eye is the lamp of the body. If your eyes are good, your
> whole body will be full of light. But if your eyes are bad, your whole
> body will be full of darkness. If then the light within you is
> darkness, how great is that darkness!
>
> No one can serve two masters. Either he will hate the one
> and love the other, or he will be devoted to the one and despise
> the other. You cannot serve both God and Money.
>
> Therefore I tell you, do not worry about your life, what you
> will eat or drink; or about your body, what you will wear. Is not
> life more important than food, and the body more important
> than clothes? Look at the birds of the air; they do not sow or
> reap or store away in barns, and yet your heavenly Father feeds
> them. Are you not much more valuable than they? Who of you by
> worrying can add a single hour to his life?
>
> And why do you worry about clothes? See how the lilies of
> the field grow. They do not labor or spin. Yet I tell you that not

even Solomon in all his splendor was dressed like one of these. If that is how God clothes the grass of the field, which is here today and tomorrow is thrown into the fire, will he not much more clothe you, O you of little faith? So do not worry, saying, "What shall we eat?" or "What shall we drink?" or "What shall we wear?" For the pagans run after all these things, and your heavenly Father knows that you need them. But seek first his kingdom and his righteousness, and all these things will be given to you as well. Therefore do not worry about tomorrow, for tomorrow will worry about itself. Each day has enough trouble of its own.

—MATTHEW 6:19–34

Little kingdom living is shaped by two points of focus. First, it is shaped by the pursuit of *earth-bound treasures* (vv. 19–24). The concept of treasure is very helpful here. A treasure is a valuable possession of any kind. As human beings we are all treasure hunters. The reason Christ's teaching here has such a ring of truth to it is because each of us in some way is a person in pursuit of some kind of treasure. Perhaps the thing of highest value to you is the affection of another. Maybe the thing of highest value to you is power and control. Or it may be a certain possession or lifestyle or experience is the treasure that you seek. Maybe it is parenting successful children or marital bliss. Perhaps it is long-term success in ministry. We all work for treasure; the only way we differ is in the kind of treasure that we seek.

Assuming that everyone seeks treasure, Christ warns against living for the physical treasures of the here and now. He warns against investing all of the gifts, talents, time, resources, and energy of your life on the impermanent and unsatisfying treasures of physical earth. But it is scary how magnetic and powerful these "treasures" are. I never wake up in the morning and say, "I want my job to be the single, life-organizing treasure of my life," but somehow it becomes that. I never say, "Today I will get my identity, meaning, and purpose from another human being," yet somehow the affection of a certain person becomes my treasure. I never say, "I have decided to find all of my personal happiness in the possession of material things," yet more and more I am living to acquire. Even though I have never made a conscious decision to make these things my treasure, the physical values of earth hook and enslave me. I never say, "I will make power and control the thing of highest value in my life," but somehow it is. I never say, "I will make the success of my children the central treasure of my life," yet somehow it happens.

In this very important teaching, Christ invites us to meditate on how sad it is for a person to invest his life in pursuit of all the wrong treasures. Then he welcomes us to humbly examine what kind of treasures we are in hot pursuit of. We weren't created to find our satisfaction in the little, earth-bound kingdom treasures of the here and now. We were created to seek a better treasure, and in so doing to be eternally grateful and satisfied.

Ask yourself: What makes your good day a good day? What are the things that tend to make you happy and satisfied? What gives your life a sense of meaning and purpose? What are the things you faithfully pursue, and what are you hoping to experience once you get them? If I watched the video of your last year, what treasure would I conclude you're after?

The second focus of little kingdom living is *anxiety-bound need* (vv. 25–34). Christ says something quite radical here. He says that you cannot reduce your life down to simply making sure all of your needs are met. Then he says, "Your life is more important than that!" You see, I was not created to shrink the size of my life to the size of my felt needs. There is something incredibly dehumanizing about living this way. If true humanity is bound up in community with God and godly community with others, I will never experience it when all my eyes ever see is my own need.

This way of living is always riddled with anxiety and fear. You see, I will never be able to control all the things that need to be controlled in order for me to guarantee that all of my needs will be met. If I am a farmer, I cannot control the weather. If I am a parent, I cannot control the hearts of my children. If I am a husband or wife, I cannot control the affection of my spouse. If I am a worker, I cannot control the economy. If I am a friend, I cannot control the acceptance of others. If I am a neighbor, I cannot control the choices of the people next door. If I am a citizen, I cannot control the powers of government. When I carry the meeting of my own needs as the most dominant focus of my living, I will always struggle with the anxiety that comes from the realization of how small the circle of my control actually is.

But there is another thing that happens here. It is the *need-expansion dynamic.* The more I focus on my needs, the more things in life get loaded into that category. The more I live with the meeting of my needs as my central focus of concern, the more things in my life get defined as needs. If you listen to the way we tend to toss around the word "need," you will soon realize how many things we have defined as needs are, in fact, not essential for life. You probably don't really "need" a good meal. You probably don't "need" a raise. You probably don't "need" that new house. You probably don't "need" the affection of that person. You probably don't "need" that position you have aspired to. You probably don't "need" to defend your reputation. You probably don't "need" the recognition of your peers. Yet, the more you focus on your own neediness, the more your desires will be christened as needs.

LOCATING THE LITTLE KINGDOM

When the Pharisees asked Jesus when the kingdom of God would come, Luke records him saying, "The kingdom of God does not come with your careful observation, nor will people say, 'Here it is,' or 'There it is,' because the kingdom of God is within you" (Luke 17:20–21). Just like the big kingdom of God, the little kingdom isn't a location, but a commitment of the heart. And because it is a commitment of the heart, I take the little kingdom with me wherever I go. So, if my heart is ruled by the *earth-bound treasures* and *anxiety-bound needs* of the little kingdom, my search for personal treasure and my quest to meet my needs will shape the way I respond to everything in my life.

In my relationships, then, I will be working to find my treasures and make sure my needs are met. At work, I will be an employee in search of treasure and need fulfillment. In ministry, I will be seeking treasure and meeting personal need. The treasure-and-need focus of the little kingdom will shape the way I interact with everything in my life. It will also shape how I feel about my life. If my relationship with a friend delivers that treasure of acceptance that I crave, then I will find that relationship enjoyable and satisfying. But if it doesn't, I will be discouraged, fearful, anxious, angry, or dissatisfied. If my work delivers the level of income that I am convinced I need, then I will enjoy my job and be motivated to invest my energies there. But if it does not, then I will feel negative about my job and find it hard to give myself to it with enthusiasm.

The little kingdom is a way of living that will shape the way I respond to everything God has placed in my life. Little kingdom living turns life into an endless search for earthly treasure and an unending focus on personal need. I sadly constrict the transcendent life that I was put on earth to enjoy to the size of my desires and needs. It is a kingdom so confined that there is no room for God or others in it. And because I was created to be part of something huge, a kingdom way bigger than the size of my life, this constricted little kingdom will crush my humanity.

Sure, I will still have relationships and I will still work. I will attend church and participate in ministry. I will involve myself in acts of giving and service. But no matter how relational and active I may seem, it is all by me and for me. It is the little kingdom, and for all the appearance of community in the way I live, there is only room for one person in it. Wherever I am and whatever I am doing, if the things that I am seeking are not to be found, it will be very hard for me to continue to participate. The little kingdom is always a kingdom of one.

SO WHY IS THE LITTLE KINGDOM SO ATTRACTIVE?

The little kingdom is attractive for one primary reason: because self is always at the center. There is a way in which this magnetizes every sinner. Sin causes each of us to be scarily self-focused. The DNA of sin is selfishness. Sin is about wanting my way, in my own way, and in my time. So, the inertia of sin is always away from others and toward self. It is there at the tree in the garden, in the deceit of Jacob, in the larceny of Achan, in the disobedience of Saul, in the treason of Absalom, in the pride of Nebuchadnezzar, in the denial of Peter, and in the treachery of Judas. It is also there in the heart of a wordless infant who stiffens his little body in anger, and in the kindergartener who taunts his classmate with the fact that his lunch is better. It is there in the catty relationships of teenagers, when I am angry because you are in my way at the grocery store, or when you eat the bowl of cereal that I had designated for my breakfast. Sin makes us want our way—our own selfish way.

The sales-pitch of the Serpent in the garden is, "You can have your own way! All you have to do is…." There is no more tempting offer to a sinner. Somewhere deep within our sinful hearts, this is what we all secretly want—our own way. And this is the thing that the Redeemer has come to rescue us from. He came to pry us from the constricted confines of our diminutive little kingdoms and, by his grace, to welcome us to the expansive glories of a better kingdom. Yet, even in the face of his grace, I will try to employ his wisdom principles and gracious promises to make my little kingdom work. You can't squeeze the large-vision lifestyle of the kingdom of God into the small-vision confines of the kingdom of self. It will simply never fit.

REMEMBERING THE FATHER AND LIVING LARGE

It was one of the hardest moments in my ministry, one that I never imagined I would ever go through. I had been one of the founders of a Christian school. I had taught there, while still being a pastor and without any additional pay. I had functioned as its principal and president of its board for eight years. Meanwhile, I had paid for each one of my children to attend. But in one shocking night, I was voted out of my position and removed from any influence over the school that was so precious to me and my ministry.

I drove home that night, unable to grasp what had actually happened. I could barely talk as I shared the horrible events of the evening with my wife. The next morning I was haunted in my thinking by the faces of the people who had led the coup. I was determined that I had to do something. I was gearing up for a fight… until I called my brother Tedd. He said, "Paul, I'm sad that this has happened to you, but what are you going to do? Are you going to go to each one of those leaders and keep going until they are convinced that they have made a mistake? Are you then going to go to every person who voted against you and do the same with them? How long do you think all of this would take? And what would happen in the process to the other things in ministry that God has called you to?"

He continued, "I know that what you are going through is very hard to face, but the school is not yours. It belongs to the Lord, and it is his to do with whatever he wants. You haven't been building your kingdom; he has been using you to build his. I suggest you get up in the morning and continue to do what God has called you to do. Serve the school and serve the people in any way you can, and entrust the health of God's kingdom into his hands."

They were tender words, but they stung. Somewhere along the way it had become *my* school. Somewhere along the way it had become about my presence and my vision. Somewhere along the way I had tried to squeeze the big kingdom vision of Christian education into the little kingdom confines of Paul Tripp's ministry. And I humbly had to admit that most of my grief was not about what was best for the school, but about the fact that they had removed me! Yes, I had been wronged, but my response to those wrongs revealed something that had happened inside of me. The two kingdoms were not only in conflict; I had confused one kingdom with another. I thought I was doing big kingdom work, but that work had begun to serve the purposes of my little kingdom visions. In a moment of painful grace, God cut a hole in my little cubicle kingdom and reached in with his loving hand and began to pull me out.

The dramatic turn in Matthew 6 doesn't come until the very end of the passage, in the second-to-last verse: "But seek first his kingdom and his righteousness, and all these things will be added to you as well." The word *but* is a welcome to a new way of living. What is the old way fueled by? The old way is driven by earth-bound treasures and anxiety-bound needs. The old way is driven by forgetting the Father and his unshakable commitment to provide all that his children need to do his kingdom work. Not much good ever comes out of functionally focusing on self, while consistently forgetting the Father.

The new way is driven by a focus on the transcendent glories of God's big kingdom purposes. Those purposes span all of history and spread to all of creation. They can never be squeezed into the constricted quarters of my little kingdom. The new way is also driven by a daily and heartfelt admission of my weakness, along with a joyful rest in the faithful provision of my Father.

Here is what we have been welcomed to: You and I can get up in the morning with a calm joy in the loving provision of our heavenly Father, while being enthralled by the fact that we have been included in the transcendent joys of his kingdom. There are glories to be enjoyed that you will never experience in the confines of your kingdom of one. You were created and called to live large. Why would you retreat into the narrow confines of your own little kingdom?

THE FINAL QUESTION: WHAT EARTH-BOUND TREASURES AND ANXIETY-BOUND NEEDS TEND TO CONTROL YOU AND YOUR RESPONSES TO LIFE?

HAVE YOU DISCOVERED...
YOUR OWN CIVILIZATION?

CHAPTER FIVE

DISCOVERING YOUR CIVILIZATION

*civ·i·li·za·tion: a type of culture or society developed
at a particular time and place*

THE BOTTOM LINE: YOU AND I ARE ALWAYS BEING CIVILIZED OR CIVILIZING OTHERS INTO THE CULTURE OF SOME KIND OF KINGDOM.

It was one of those great Discovery Channel specials. Archeologists were working to uncover data about a certain battle that had been recorded in the annals of history, but about which physical proof had never been found. As they began their dig, they immediately began to uncover evidence of conflict. At first they were jubilant at how easily and quickly the discovery had come. But the more they dug, the more they became confused. The more they examined the artifacts that they now held in their hands, the more they were convinced that this was not the battle site for which they had been searching. Now, they really began to get excited. They had no idea what they were looking at.

The power of the discovery began to grip them. Perhaps they had done it. Perhaps they were in the midst of uncovering a civilization previously unknown. Little did they know that what they were about to uncover would forever change the world's view of the history of this region. They hadn't proven their battle theory, but they had uncovered a whole new civilization!

This is what I want to do with you in this chapter. I want to take you with me on an archeological dig into the civilization of the sinful human heart. I want us to examine the pottery shards that lie there. I want us to hold artifacts of the heart in our hands and examine them with our eyes.

YOU'RE MORE CIVILIZED THAN YOU THINK

In the last chapter we talked about the fact that we are all kingdom builders. Another way of saying this is that we are all *civilizers*. We all are at work building some kind of society or culture. We either give ourselves to building the culture of self, or we joyfully participate in building the culture of the King. Every day is shaped by the blueprints, laws, policies, structures, plans, politics, relationships, goals, purposes, and actions of some kind of civilization. If you are a human being you cannot escape this work. You and I are always being "civilized" and civilizing others into the culture of some kind of kingdom. When children are stuck in traffic with their irate father as he curses the existence of the auto-bound human beings who are in his way, they are being civilized into a way of thinking and responding to life. When a teenage boy mocks a classmate to gain status with his peers, he is civilizing his target. When a mother lovingly teaches her children how to live at peace with one another, they are being civilized. When a wife, in quest of material ease, spends their family into serious debt, she is civilizing her mate. When a pastor unfolds the transcendent glory of God before the people of his church, he is civilizing his hearers. We are always working to build some kind of civilization, and we are always pressing the rules and values of that civilization onto others. Let me give you an easy example.

Let's pretend that there is a mother for whom the possession of fine material things is one of the highest values in her little kingdom of one. Her teenage son has been learning the rules of his mother's material kingdom for years. He has learned to maintain his bedroom as if it were a museum and to never walk on the hardwood floors with his shoes on. He has learned to wash the car, even when to him it simply didn't look dirty. He has learned to never invite a friend home without giving his mom plenty of notice. He has learned the kitchen is to look like it has never been eaten in, and that he must always dress like he just stepped out of a Gap ad. None of these rules has been written down, but they are the understood values of the culture of his home. You see, this teenager has been civilized by the rules of his mother's little kingdom. But now he is in real trouble. He has just confessed that he has wrecked her new car, and in his nervousness he has also spilled soda on her new white sofa. In his mother's kingdom, there is no room for either thing; now he is in the crosshairs of her anger.

It's not just that we all tend to build our own little claustrophobic kingdoms, but that we want the people who are around us to keep the rules of our kingdoms as well. So, we all have ways of enculturating the people around us. The engaged woman enculturates her fiancé in the rules of her kingdom by inflicting him with silence when he doesn't give her the compliments that she seeks. After four or five of these moments of silence, he learns the rules and the necessity of keeping them. The father, who wants peace and quiet in the house while he is reading the paper, enculturates his family by his angry outbursts. Before long, they all learn to tiptoe around him when he has the newspaper in his hands. The boss who is obsessed with his own success enculturates his employees in the rules of his kingdom by a system of threats and rewards.

Before long each of his employees is "civilized" and toes the line as demanded. The junior high kids enculturate their peer into their civilization of appearance, by their mocking laughter when he wears something that is not approved. He learns the rules quickly, quits letting his mom choose his clothes for him, and determines to only wear what is on the "cool" list.

In each example, people are being civilized—that is, taught the rules of the little kingdom and told what will happen if they don't stay within those rules. There is a way in which all of us want the people around us to serve the purposes of our kingdoms. We are all building some kind of civilization, and we are all civilizing the people around us.

BLIND AND CONFUSED

One of the problems in what we have been considering is that all of this profound, life-shaping kingdom building takes place in the context of the utterly mundane. Your kingdom building always takes place in small and little-noticed moments because that's where you live. No one ever says to another person, "I am building a kingdom to myself, and if you want to have a relationship with me you have to be willing to keep the rules of my kingdom." No one ever says, "I have decided to forsake the glories of the kingdom of God to pursue the self-oriented glories of my own kingdom." Instead, because of the blindness of sin and the fact that we exist in little moments, so much of our kingdom building takes place without conscious intentionality. And because we have defined biblical morality as the keeping of a set of rules, rather than the ownership of our hearts by the Lord, much of the conflict of kingdoms goes unnoticed. As a result, our lives end up being shaped by a confusing mix of big kingdom rules (the kingdom of God) and little kingdom rules (the kingdom of self).

In the home, dad doesn't only get angry when God's law is broken, but when his law is broken as well. Mom isn't only dedicated to seeing her children internalize God's standards; she wants them to internalize the rules of her civilization as well. The child's experience is that breaking the little kingdom rules get as much attention as breaking the big kingdom rules, and sometimes even more. In the blender of the frenetic schedule of the average modern Christian family, these two systems of law get so mixed up it becomes hard to separate one from the other. We say we are serving God, but there is another civilization that is shaping every intention, decision, and action.

When it comes to which kingdom we are building, it is very easy to be blind and confused. We say we embrace the transcendent, but where the rubber meets the road in our daily lives, our living shrinks to the field of our personal concerns. We don't forsake the faith, but the real kingdom we are building, where we live and work each day, is a kingdom of one.

THE CHARACTERISTICS OF THE CIVILIZATION OF SELF

Because of the subtle deceptiveness of our kingdom building attempts to enculturate others, it is important that we recognize what the little kingdom looks like. None of us tends to think that we are living for ourselves. The presence of the civilization of self is just that subtle. We all tend to credit ourselves with living for God. Sadly, the truth for most of us is that our living is shaped by a troublesome mix of the agenda of the two kingdoms. We can do big kingdom things (ministry to others) with little kingdom motives (for respect or acceptance). Or we can do both at the same time (I serve you, while telling you how mad I've been at you for something you did to me). We must remember that the inertia of sin is always away from the big kingdom and toward the little kingdom. This conflict between kingdoms is the war of wars. It is what spiritual warfare is all about.

The problem is that the greatest battles take place in the smallest moments, so its moral drama can go almost unnoticed. And it is possible for God's people to walk around spiritually maimed and not even know it. It is possible for us to profess allegiance to the big kingdom and yet, in our daily choices, be fighting for the success of the kingdom of one. So, identifying the characteristics of the little kingdom is very important. Let me list and discuss them with you.

Self-focus. This is what we have been discussing all along. The little kingdom *is* a kingdom of self. It is driven by personal desire and need. Its eyes are always inward, and its rules are determined by what is best for me. It squeezes all of my relationships and activities into the contours of my felt needs and personal treasures. Even though I may not know I am doing it, I will enter every forum of my life with a "what's in it for me" posture. I will like you when you are helping me get what I want, but I will struggle with spontaneous anger toward you when you unwittingly get in the way of what I want. Although I may describe myself as a God-fearer, I functionally sit in the center of my universe. The single most influential focus of the little kingdom is its focus on self. What is "good" for me is the law of this universe of one. *Whose "good" drives your daily conversations, decisions, and actions?*

Self-righteousness. Only when I focus on the holiness and glory of God am I able to see myself with accuracy. Self-righteousness blinds me to the realities of who I am and tends to make me much more aware of the sin of others than my own. I will be angry with others, not because they sin, but because in their sin they get in the way of what I am convinced I need. Since no one is more influential in my life than me, and because no one talks to me more than I do, what I say to myself about myself is very important. The little kingdom, being more dominated by my internal conversation than by God's revelation, does not encourage a humble and accurate view of self. Instead, my view of myself is colored by two things: arguments for my righteousness ("I did this for them") and plausible lies that cover my sin ("It wasn't gossip; I just thought they should know so they could pray"). It is scary, but you can joyfully sing about grace on Sunday and yet during the week you can be involved in patterns of self-atonement that make whatever you are doing acceptable to your conscience. *Whose righteousness gives you courage and hope as you deal with daily life?*

Self-satisfaction. The big question of the little kingdom is, "Am I satisfied with my life?" My dad used to say, "This just drives me crazy!" He was basically saying, "I'm not satisfied, and you better do something about it!" Let me remind you that all of this takes place in the little moments where we live every day. The big question of the little kingdom is not, "Is God honored by my life?" Nor is it, "By his grace, have I lived up to his purpose and according to his design?" And the little kingdom definitely does not ask, "Have I loved God above all else and my neighbor as myself?" No, the little kingdom only asks one question: "Am I satisfied with myself and my life?" If I am satisfied with me, then all is well in the kingdom of one. *Whom are you seeking to satisfy?*

Self-reliance. The culture of the little kingdom is not a culture of humble community with God and others. In this kingdom, I don't move toward others with a sense of spiritual interdependency with them. You see, self-righteousness always leads to self-reliance. To the degree that I have convinced myself that I am righteous, I free myself of the need for God and others. In the kingdom of one, I live for my own purpose and by my own strength. The kingdom of one is about being strong and in control. The kingdom of one is never a kingdom of spiritual weakness, neediness, and grace. *Do you live in humble daily community with God and others, admitting your need and seeking help?*

Self-rule. The highest law in the little kingdom is the law of self. It makes sense that when I am living for self I become a law unto myself. I make up the standards by which I evaluate me and judge others. The highest will of the kingdom of one is the will of self. In this kingdom, what I have determined I need will always become the highest moral value. *I* determine what I wish to experience. In this kingdom I love me and have a wonderful plan for my life. *Whose rules get the most attention and the quickest response in your life and relationships?*

Self-glorification. The daily war between these kingdoms is a battle between competing glories. Will our hearts be ruled by the shadow glories of physical earth or by the one glory that is worthy of the title, the glory of God? As sinners we are magnetized toward pursuing our personal definitions of glory. Often, under the veneer of theological beliefs and participation in the public life of the church, the true glory we are living for is the glory of self. *Whose glory motivates you to do what you do and to say what you say?*

BUT WAIT, THERE IS A WARRIOR!

Yes, there is grace for this battle! In the person and work of Jesus Christ, God has made ample provision for you and me as we live with kingdoms in conflict. His grace blows a hole in your self-contained kingdom, and in his redemptive love he reaches in and pulls you out, again and again. Paul says it this way: "He has delivered us from the domain of darkness and transferred us to the kingdom of his beloved son, in whom we have redemption, the forgiveness of sins" (Colossians 1:13–14, ESV). Let's consider what God has given us for the war we are considering.

On the cross Christ broke the power of the little kingdom. (See Romans 6:1–14.) As God's children we no longer live under the domination of the little kingdom. We have been freed from our imprisonment to ourselves. Once we were only able to desire, think, speak, and act in a self-focused way, but now grace has broken that slavery and welcomed us to a new and better way of living. Christ endured the awful suffering and death of the cross, not just to ensure your future with him in eternity, but to *free* you in the here and now to live for something more transcendent than your present definition of personal happiness. The cross smashed the dominant power of the shadow glories of creation over your heart and freed your heart to run after the transcendent glory that you will only find in him. Yes, you can escape the stultifying confines of your little civilization and live in the big sky country of his kingdom where you live and work each day.

On the cross Christ paid the debt for every selfish desire, thought, word, or deed to which you will ever give yourself. You no longer have to be afraid to own up to your selfishness. You do not have to whitewash your thoughts and motives. You do not have to cover your sin by blaming others or by self-atoning logic. You do not have to give yourself to acts of penance (self-atonement) that make you feel better about yourself. You do not have to search for biblical passages that will give ease to your conscience. No, your debt has been fully paid. Your punishment has been borne by Another. There is One who has taken your place and been condemned instead of you. Paul says, "He forgave us all our sins, having canceled the written code, with its regulations, that was against us and that stood opposed to us; he took it away, nailing it to the cross" (Colossians 2:13b–14). As God's child, you have been forgiven for every act of self-focused independence and rebellion. You have been freed from the debt of your every failure to love God above all else and your neighbor as yourself. You no longer need to live in hiding. Forgiving grace welcomes you out of the darkness to lift the burden of refusal, guilt, fear, and shame off of your shoulders. You have been invited to confess and receive the forgiveness that is yours.

On the cross Christ purchased power for you to obey. Although the *power* of the little kingdom over your heart has been broken, the *presence* of little kingdom thoughts and desires still remains. So, the cross has purchased daily power for you. Paul says, "And having disarmed the powers and authorities, he made a public spectacle of them, triumphing over them by the cross" (Colossians 2:15). You can stand and say, "No!" to the self-focused agenda of the little kingdom. In that moment at work, or in the family room, over the fence with the neighbor, at supper with friends, in the situation of parental discipline, or in a discussion with your spouse, you have not been left to your own strength. You have been given power beyond what you can imagine! Listen to what Paul says to the struggling Ephesian Christians: "Now to him who is able to do immeasurably more than all we ask or imagine, according to his power that is at work *within us*" (Ephesians 3:20, author's emphasis). One of the results of the cross of Jesus Christ is the gift of the Holy Spirit. Think about it. God in his awesome power and glory has come to live inside of you. Because of this you are able to be who he has called you to be and do what he has called you to do, even in the face of the powerful temptations you encounter in this fallen world. And his power is without limit, so that you not only have the potential to live for his big kingdom once, but over and over again. His presence in your heart guarantees your potential to endure.

The cross of Christ guarantees that some day your kingdom conflict will be over. There is a time of peace coming, and it will last forever! There will be a day when you are no longer tricked and tempted by an evil and deceitful enemy. There will be a day when your life will no longer be a battleground. There will be a day when you will no longer have to confess your failure or plead for help. There will be a day when you will no longer have to examine every thought and evaluate every motive. One day the little kingdom will be finally and forever crushed, never to rise again. In that day, a joyful and satisfied desire for the glory of God will rule the hearts of everyone. The great war of wars—that great conflict of kingdoms that has been played out on the heart of every person who ever lived—will someday be over. The kingdom of God will win! The King of kings will rule! Peace will come!

Until then, the battle of kingdoms goes on. This battle couldn't be more practical in its focus. God couldn't love us and leave us to our little civilization of self, because when self is at the center, God no longer occupies center stage. As David Henderson says,

> Because God no longer occupies center stage, terms like self-love, self-expression, self-confidence, and self-fulfillment, none of which graces the pages of the Scriptures, begin to dominate

the church's conversation. Meanwhile other "self" words straight from the Bible like self-surrender, self-sacrifice, self-denial, and self-control slip into disuse. Self, great big and smack dab in the middle, squeezes out the notions of a holy God, a fallen self, an undeserved gift of grace in Jesus Christ, and a divine call on one's whole life. When this happens, we may be preaching, we may be sharing faith, but what we are communicating (or this author would add, what we are living) is not genuine Christianity. In Christianity, the one place the self cannot be is at the center. That is the rightful place of God alone.[1]

So, your Lord battles on your behalf, and he will never rest until the battle is over. Why don't you commit yourself right now to be one of his soldiers? Start by looking for the civilizing of self in your own life. Ask yourself the questions at the end of each characteristic of the little kingdom above. Affirm your forgiveness by coming out of hiding and confessing your faults. Then affirm your identity as the temple where the Spirit dwells, and step forward in courage to live a new way. You can enjoy the fresh air of grace and the transcendent vistas of glory that are yours to experience in the kingdom of God. If you are his child, his cross has made you a citizen of this civilization of glory and grace. Why would you go back to your own little kingdom?

THE FINAL QUESTION: IN WHAT WAYS DO YOU TRY TO GET THE PEOPLE AROUND YOU TO FOLLOW THE RULES OF YOUR KINGDOM OF SELF?

WHAT MASK DOES
YOUR KINGDOM WEAR?

CHAPTER SIX

THE COSTUME KINGDOM

*mas·quer·ade: to pretend to be someone or
something that you are not*

THE BOTTOM LINE: THE MOST DANGEROUS THING ABOUT THE KINGDOM OF SELF IS HOW EASILY IT MASQUERADES AS THE KINGDOM OF GOD.

It was always one of the most dramatic moments in this well-known secret agent drama. Although viewers didn't know it, one of the *Mission Impossible* agents had donned a latex mask that was meant to make him look familiar and safe to the enemy. The mask was so pliable and real-looking that it took on the appearance of actual human skin. At some crucial moment, the government agent would reach up and tear the "skin" off his face and reveal his true identity to the international bad guys who were about to be taken down. As a child, I loved watching those moments. I dreamed of growing up and being the latex mask agent. I imagined what it would be like to reach up and tear off my face to the surprise of bad guys who were plotting evil. I imagined that much secret agent work was done in costume and that most of our spies had a collection of the appropriate latex masks at their disposal. I really did want to be part of this government-sponsored costume kingdom. And I wanted to be the costume king.

As a sinner, I am still seeking to be the king of a costume kingdom. You see, the problem with the little kingdom (the civilization of self) is that it dresses up and puts on the mask of the big kingdom (the kingdom of God). It puts on the mask of things that are righteous and good, while it is capturing the heart for the glory of self. The most dangerous kinds of self-focus are those that take on the form of the good things of the kingdom of God. Indian theologian Vinoth Ramachandra describes it this way:

> The Good News is packaged and marketed (using, uncritically, all the techniques of modern advertising) as a religious product: offering "peace of mind", "how to get to heaven", heath and prosperity", "inner healing", "the answer to all your problems" etc. What is promoted as "faith in God" often turns out to be a means for obtaining emotional security or material blessing in this life and an insurance policy in the next. This kind of preaching leaves the status quo untouched. It does not raise fundamental and disturbing questions about the assumptions upon which people build their lives. It does not threaten the false gods in whose name the creation of God has been taken over; indeed it actually reinforces their hold on their worshippers. This kind of "gospel" is essentially escapist, the direct descendent of the pseudo-gospels of the false prophets of the Old Testament. It is simply a religious image of the secular consumerist culture in which modern men and women live.[1]

There are many warnings in the Bible about the costuming of the kingdom of self. Christ makes this warning in the Sermon on the Mount: "Watch out for false prophets. They come to you in sheep's clothing, but inwardly they are ferocious wolves" (Matthew 7:15). Paul writes to Christians in Corinth: "For such men are false apostles, deceitful workmen, masquerading as apostles of Christ. And no wonder, for Satan himself masquerades as an angel of light. It is not surprising then, if his servants masquerade as servants of righteousness. Their end will be what their actions deserve" (2 Corinthians 11:13–15). In Philippians 1:15–16, Paul talks about people who even preach the gospel for their own selfish ends! In Galatians, Paul warns against a false gospel that wears the costume of the true gospel. Notice the strong language: "I am astonished that you are so quickly deserting the one who called you by the grace of Christ and are turning to a different gospel—which is really no gospel at all. Evidently some people are throwing you into confusion and are trying to pervert the gospel of Christ." And then, just in case his warning wasn't strong enough he says, "But even if we or an angel from heaven should preach a gospel other than the one we preached to you, let him be eternally condemned!" (Galatians 1:6–8).

Why is Paul so agitated? Because the kingdom of self is most dangerous when it takes on the contours of the kingdom of God. It is quite possible for you to be convinced that you are living for the transcendent glories of the kingdom of God when you are, in fact, living for yourself. Be warned! Be scared! The little kingdom is a costume kingdom, and it is deviously promoted by a costume king—Satan himself. The little kingdom will quite regularly don the latex masks of outward participation in worship, obedience, and ministry. It will appear as though it is serving the King of kings and Lord of lords, when daily it is bowing before the throne of self. Driven by earth-bound treasures and anxiety-bound needs, its worship can only be the worship of self. As Ramachandra says,

> This kind of religion, whether in Christian or other forms, is *idolatry* by biblical definition. For at the heart of idolatry is the attempt to manipulate "God" or the unseen "spiritual world" in

order to obtain security and well-being for oneself and one "group" (whether family, business corporation, ethnic community, or nation-state). Biblical faith, in contrast, is the radical abandonment of our whole being in grateful trust and love to the God disclosed in the life, death and resurrection of Jesus Christ: so that we become willing agents in a costly confrontation with every form of evil and unjust suffering in the world. This faith involves us in embracing the pain and confusion of others, and in being willing to live with uncertainty ourselves while moving towards a future that is *already at work among us.*[2]

It is very important to note that the most dangerous idols for all of us are those that are easily Christianized. Selfishness is most dangerous when it masquerades as service. Self-focus is most powerful when it dons the costume of love. Earthly treasures are most seductive when they take on the appearance of spiritual need. Idols do their nastiest work when they wear the latex mask of God. Because the little kingdom is a costume kingdom, it presents a near and present danger to everyone who has committed himself to the kingdom of God.

THE FRUIT OF THE COSTUME KINGDOM

If you examine the church of Jesus Christ in our day, the visible location of the big kingdom, it won't be long before you see the fruit of the little kingdom. Think of it this way. Suppose I have committed myself to a healthful diet, and I am at least externally keeping its rules. At the same time, however, I am sneaking in copious amounts of chocolate chip cookies. Two things will surely result from this pattern. First, the cookies in the jar will begin to mysteriously disappear. Second, I will gain weight rather than lose it. Now, it is quite obvious that neither of these results is the fruit of a healthful diet, which points to the fact that what has masqueraded as a diet is not a diet at all, but an even more deceptive form of overeating.

If you look around in your life and the lives of fellow Christians, you will see fruit that is not the result of a joyful commitment to the transcendent glories of God's kingdom. Instead, these things are the fruit of serving the self, while masquerading as living for the King. Bad fruit results because "less" has taken on the costume of "more." In a very illusive way, the transcendent glories of the kingdom of God have been shrunk down to the size of my earth-bound treasures and my anxiety-bound needs. It is not the fruit of remembering the Father and being freed to give myself to his kingdom. No, it is the fruit of forgetting the Father and making sure that I actually get what I have told myself I need. And remember, all this takes place in the form of worship, obedience, and ministry.

Let's consider three things that are the fruit of the kingdom of self hiding out in the kingdom of God.

A lack of excitement and enthusiasm in the gospel. It is amazing how casual we can be about the glory of the gospel! Surely some of this is the result of familiarity, but as I examine my own life and spend time with others, I am convinced that something deeper is operating here. When the gospel (being welcomed into God's presence to live for his glory) is no longer the end, but a means to an end, then my enthusiasm will not be for the gospel, but for the "stuff" that I think it will give me. So, for example, I may be grateful for the gospel, but what really excites me is the hope that my relationship with God will give me what I really want, such as the marriage of my dreams.

As a new Christian, Drew seemed to have an insatiable love for the things of the Lord. He could not find enough Bible studies. He read as many Christian books as he could get his hands on. He took copious notes during every sermon. His presence seemed to open and close almost every gathering of his church. Now, five years later, Drew seems to be a different man. The sermon notebook doesn't accompany him to worship services anymore. He seldom attends the gatherings of his small group, and he is barely able to get himself up in time to have a brief personal time of worship before he hits his day.

What happened to Drew? The same thing that happens to many believers. Drew came to Christ as a lonely young man. Although he did not know it, his enthusiasm for the gospel was not about the grace and glory of Christ. No, in the church Drew had found the circle of friends he had always longed to have. In the church, Drew had found a family. And while that is very good, the spiritual problem was that the end (a love relationship with Christ) had functionally become the means to another end (acceptance with a family of people). Big kingdom glories were a way to experience little kingdom treasures.

And these relationships with sinners proved to be flawed, as they always will be this side of heaven. Eventually, Drew's growing lack of enthusiasm for the gospel revealed that his excitement about his newfound faith was simply the kingdom of self dressed up in the costume of the kingdom of God.

Disappointment with God and/or Christianity. In almost thirty years of counseling, I cannot tell you how many believers I have encountered who were either disappointed with God or disillusioned with Christianity. I have endeavored over the years to carefully and patiently listen to their stories. And, although each story is unique and different, there has been one theme running through them all. Their disappointment with God or Christianity is not that God has failed in his faithfulness or love or that the teachings of Scripture have not proven to be true. No, they are disappointed because they thought that God's love and the principles of Scripture would result in certain things in their lives. When these things failed to materialize, it was hard not to be disappointed.

Marylynn stated it most clearly when, after her divorce from her unrepentant husband she said, "Frankly, Paul, when I came to Christ, this is not what I signed on for." The Psalms are in the Bible to confront the Marylynn in us all. In the Psalms, the life of faith isn't idyllic, pretty, or easy. It is a walk with God marked by anguish, dread, and grief. The

Psalms picture a life where prayers seem to go unanswered, where God seems distant, and where evil seems to be winning. The Psalms welcome us to a faith where God's agenda is more important than ours and where we are asked to live out our faith in the context of a disastrously broken world. But this is also precisely where we experience the highest personal joys, as we put our hope in the covenant love of the Lord and make the pursuit of his glory the goal of our lives.

We will tend to take on the image of our little kingdom treasures. Listen to the words of Psalm 115:1–8.

> Not to us, O LORD, not to us
> > but to your name be the glory,
> > because of your love and faithfulness.
> Why do the nations say,
> > "Where is their God?"
> Our God is in heaven;
> > he does whatever pleases him.
> But their idols are silver and gold,
> > made by the hands of men.
> They have mouths, but cannot speak,
> > eyes, but they cannot see;
> they have ears, but cannot hear,
> > noses, but they cannot smell;
> they have hands, but cannot feel,
> > feet, but they cannot walk;
> > nor can they utter a sound with their throats.
> Those who make them will be like them,
> > and so will all who trust in them.

Psalm 115 teaches many things, but one of the most important is this principle: *you become like the treasure that you seek.* It is an eloquent and accurate principle. When I live for material things, I increasingly become a materialistic person. I start to care about things more than people, thus becoming like the things I crave. Similarly, the person who lives for the little kingdom treasure of control will inevitably become a power-obsessed, controlling person. Someone who gets his identity and meaning from relationships will become driven by what people think of him, living in unending fear of man.

Rather than developing the traits of Christian character, which are the result of pursuing and treasuring Christ, I will take on the qualities of my Christ-replacement. This is why so many people in our churches are not growing in Christlikeness. To the degree that Jesus is not the treasure I seek, I will not be progressively taking on his likeness. Instead, I will begin to look more and more like the treasure of the kingdom of self that I am actually living for.

It was by far the most disappointing party of my childhood. We were all told that there would be prizes for the best costume of the night. My dad was pretty creative when it came to costumes, and my mom was a good seamstress. As a result, they helped me create a killer costume. With great excitement, I went to that party dressed as a very convincing old lady. What I didn't know until I arrived at the party was that you weren't allowed to take off your mask until someone had discovered who you really were. Well, my costume was so well-executed that it completely disguised my true identity. No one could figure out who I was! But as the night wore on, it became quite clear that the children who had been discovered and who had taken off their costumes were the ones having all the fun. I spent the night sitting on a chair watching the fun proceed until finally, by the process of elimination, someone figured out who I was.

TAKING OFF THE MASK

These three things—lack of excitement with the gospel, disappointment with God and with Christianity, and taking on the traits of my treasure rather than the character of Christ—can rip the mask off of the costume kingdom in your life. Could it be that you have shrunk the kingdom of God down to the size of your little kingdom treasures? Could it be that your excitement with the things of the Lord is not really about the Lord at all? Could it be that the transcendent glory of God and his kingdom has become for you more of a means to an end rather than the end itself?

The scary thing about the kingdom of self is that it is a costume kingdom. It very quickly takes on the shape and appearance of the kingdom of God. It is very easy to think that we are living for God, while our personal agenda still rules our hearts and shapes our decisions, words, and actions. It is very easy to think that we are living for the transcendent joys of intimate communion with God, fueled by a personal enthusiasm for his glory, when in fact we have placed our hope in the shadow glories of this created world. It is very easy to think that we have exited the narrow confines of our little cubicle kingdoms to breathe the spiritually invigorating air of the kingdom of God, when really we are more entrapped in our cubicles than ever before. It is very easy for our earth-bound treasures and anxiety-bound needs to masquerade as love for Christ and enthusiasm for his work on earth. It is very easy to shrink the size of your life to the size of your life and not know it, because the little kingdom of self has been a costume kingdom since the time of the fatal deception in the garden.

THE COSTUME KINGDOM AND THE ONE TRUE KING

Be honest with yourself. What *are* you after? What *are* you living for? Is there a place in your life where your little kingdom purposes have been masquerading as the kingdom of God? Has your life with God shrunk to the size of "me and mine"? What in your life right now really excites you? What things do you find fulfilling and satisfying? What has become your treasure, and how do you define your needs? Is there a place where selfishness wears the latex mask of godliness? Is your little kingdom so well costumed that no one around you would ever recognize it for what it really is? What kingdom owns your heart where you live and work each day?

And as you ask yourself these questions, remember that on a Sabbath day long ago your Redeemer stood up in the synagogue and quoted these words from Isaiah, applying them to himself.

> The Spirit of the Lord is on me,
>   because he has anointed me
>   to preach good news to the poor.
> He has sent me to proclaim freedom for the prisoners
>   and recovery of sight for the blind,
> to release the oppressed,
>   to proclaim the year of the Lord's favor.
>   —Luke 4:18–19

You are not alone in this battle to unmask and dismantle the little kingdom in your life. Be excited! Your Messiah gives you just what you need for this battle. The little kingdom leaves you poor, so he offers you the good news of the eternal riches of his grace. The little kingdom enslaves you, so he endured the cross to set you free. The little kingdom leaves you blind, so he places hands of grace on you to restore your sight. The little kingdom has left you oppressed, so he purchased your release. In your Lord you find all the resources you need to live with insight and liberty while you breathe the big sky air of his glorious kingdom.

Your hope and mine will not be found in another kingdom. What we all desperately need is a King who will liberate us from the kingdoms we build to ourselves. That King has come for you and for me, and Emmanuel, the Lord *Jesus* Christ, is his name. Seek him! There is help to be found!

THE FINAL QUESTION: IN YOUR EVERYDAY LIFE
RIGHT NOW, WHERE ARE YOU TELLING YOURSELF
THAT YOU ARE LIVING FOR GOD
WHEN YOU ARE REALLY LIVING FOR YOURSELF?

HAVE YOU SHRUNK YOUR LIFE TO THE SIZE OF YOUR LIFE?

CHAPTER SEVEN

THE SHRINK DYNAMIC

*dy·nam·ic: an interactive system or process,
characterized by action or forcefulness*

THE BOTTOM LINE: SIN CAUSES ALL OF US TO SHRINK THE SIZE OF OUR LIVES TO THE SIZE OF OUR LIVES.

Unless you're an alien from another planet, you've probably been frustrated by it. It was created by the French scientist Henri DePoix to preserve meat for soldiers during the World War I. It is simply plastic that has had its molecules stretched under high temperatures and then cooled. The soldiers' meat was preserved, so we've been finding uses for it ever since. It makes it nearly impossible for you to open your child's new toy, or that CD you can't wait to listen to, or the pocket knife you just bought at the hardware store. We use it to protect antique books and the ski boat between seasons. You know it well, because you've encountered it many times. It's called "shrink wrap."

The amazing thing about shrink wrap is that it does it every time without fail. It is one of the most successful and predictable products ever invented. It will always shrink to the exact size of whatever it has been wrapped around. Whether it's a piece of beef jerky or dad's prize fishing boat, it always shrinks to the contour of the thing inside of it, and it's always difficult to take it off. Henri DePoix had no idea how his commission to keep soldiers from food poisoning would change the life of every modern consumer.

The effect of sin is very similar to DePoix's invention, but its influence is much more comprehensive. Sin causes fundamental changes in the "molecules" of my heart. No longer is my heart driven by a deep-seated love for God. No longer is my heart motivated by a genuine care for others. No longer do I carry around a sense of responsibility for the surrounding created world. No longer is every decision I make shaped by a clear sense of what is morally right and morally wrong. No longer is everything I do shaped by joyful and thankful worship. The DNA of sin is selfishness, and it shrinks the size of my universe to the size of one. Sin creates the ultimate *shrink dynamic*. It causes all of us in some way to shrink the size of our lives to the size of our lives. Sin shrinks my motivation, zeal, desire, care, and concern to the contours of my life. In the shrunken kingdom of self, there is no functional room for God or others. It is humbling, but spiritually essential, to admit that sin has shrink-wrapped us all.

You see it in a wordless infant who in the crib stiffens his body in anger, because his mother has had the audacity to leave the room. You see it in the endless fights of young children over who had the toy first or who hit whom first. You see it in the endless repetition of a teenager's self-centered complaints. You see it in the hardships of the first few years of marriage, when the newlyweds are shocked by what it takes to live in a loving relationship with another human being. You see it in how difficult it is for the people of a church to be unified. You see it in drivers racing for a parking spot. You see it in a million moments of human covetousness and envy. You see it in broken families and crime-ridden cities. You see it in the bitter complaints of the old man as his life ebbs away. Sin atrophies our care and shrinks our concern. No matter how you dress it up, the news isn't really that good: sin leaves us caring about little more than ourselves. It is a condition in which we were simply not made to live.

Since the Bible records the damage of sin and the need for redemption, this *shrink dynamic* is illustrated throughout biblical history. Think about it. Adam and Eve shrunk the size of their lives to the size of their desire to be like God. Cain shrunk the size of his life to the size of his desire to have what Abel had. Jacob shrunk the size of his life to the size of his quest for Esau's inheritance. The children of Israel in the wilderness shrunk the size of their lives to the size of their desire for better food (than manna). Achan shrunk the size of his life to the size of his lust for Palestinian plunder. King Saul shrunk the size of his life to the size of his craving for the spoils of the Amalekite defeat. Jonah shrunk the size of his life to the size of his own definition of justice. The Pharisees shrunk the size of their lives to the size of their own righteousness. Peter shrunk the size of his life to the size of his fear of others. Judas shrunk the size of his life to the size of thirty pieces of silver. These are but a few of the biblical stories that chronicle how sin shrinks our hearts to care for little more than ourselves.

BROKEN MODELS, SELFISH DESIRES

It was one of my worst childhood moments. My brother Tedd had quite the prestigious model car collection, carefully displayed on shelves in his bedroom. He had assembled and painted them all himself and was quite proud of his handiwork. For some reason that I don't now remember, Tedd had angered me. He made the mistake of breaking my law, so in a fit of anger, I hit him where I knew it would hurt. I ran into his room, took off my shoe, and smashed his collection. I knew what I was doing, and it felt good. Well, it felt good until my mom discovered what I had done.

This sad moment in the life of one child is a picture of every sinner. We all want to be accepted, served, and validated by the people and circumstances around us. When this doesn't happen, our reactions range from mild irritation to violent anger. Married couples criticize one another, not because their spouse has broken God's law, but their own law. Parents get angry with their children, not because they are sinners, but because in their sin they mess up what their parents crave. Neighbors break relationship with each other because they don't like the way they have been treated or the way the neighbor keeps his yard. Businessmen work too hard and too long because they are never able to be satisfied and content. People move in and out of local churches as if they were malls because they didn't feel like they were getting what they needed. Siblings fight over the final bowl of cereal, who gets to hold the remote control, where people are going to sit in the car, and who gets to take his shower first. People at parties jockey to be the center of attention. A man will throw a good marriage away for a few moments of erotic pleasure, and a teenager will sell his soul for the acceptance of his peers.

People live with a debt load they are unable to bear because they have convinced themselves that they need more than they really need. We think our houses aren't big enough, that there aren't enough clothes in our closet, and that we haven't got enough money in our pockets. We eat much more than we need and talk about being hungry when we seldom actually experience what the word means. We constantly think "me and mine," "bigger and better," and "now not later." We hate it when someone is in the bathroom we want to use, when we're asked to do something we hadn't planned on, or when we are asked to go without. We think getting is a greater blessing than giving. We love it when we are able to prove ourselves right and another wrong. We dream of what our lives would be like if we were in control. We are often blind to opportunities to love, while we are all too skilled at remembering an offense against us.

Everywhere you look you see it. The implications are impossible to escape. It makes it hard for us to live with one another and nearly impossible to be content within ourselves. The fundamental core of sin is selfishness. It is a solitary universe turned in on itself. Sin really is the ultimate shrink wrap. It shrinks the size of your care and concern to the contours of your life. From the little boy in anger smashing his brother's model cars to the wife who is bitter because she never got the marriage of her dreams, sin does something tragic. It turns us in on ourselves. Stop, look, and listen, and you will see the tendency in you and around you.

THE HUGE CONTOURS OF GOD

What's so heinous about all of this is that when I am content to live in my little kingdom of one, it is God who gets squeezed out. He will not shrink himself to the size of my solitary kingdom. He cannot abandon his only glory or deny his sovereign plan. He will be God, and he will not be anything else. The kingdom that is to capture and motivate us was meant to be no smaller than the size of his grandeur. I was never meant to shrink the size of my life to a size smaller than the contours of his glory. I was never created to establish my own kingdom, but to give myself in wholehearted, sacrificial devotion to his.

The psalmist in Psalm 145 captures the expansiveness of this kind of living with a picturesque phrase. He says that the greatness of God no one can fathom. A fathom is a measurement of water depth. When something is fathomless, it means it is so great that it cannot be measured. It has no bottom to it. The psalmist is basically saying that if you lined up every human being who has ever lived, and if they each dug down into God's greatness, one after another, they would still not come to the bottom of it! His glory is just that deep. The size of my living was meant to be connected to the depth of his greatness. The fathomless greatness of God *is* the more that I was designed to live for.

When I expand my living inside the huge tent of his glory, immediately there is room for other people in my life as well. Community with him results in meaningful community with others. Think about it. Sin is functionally atheistic and antisocial. Because it reduces my focus to me, it blinds me both to God and to others. And as a sinner, I may participate in formal religion and conduct relationships with others, but only to the degree that they fit with the purposes of my solitary kingdom. When I do this, there is no real room for worship of God and love for others in my functional life plan. Worship and love, wherever they exist in my life, get shrunk to the size of what I think I need and what I have determined I want. Whatever religion or community exists in my life, what I am really worshipping is me. So I will sing praise to God's faithfulness on Sunday, yet question his goodness on Tuesday when he doesn't deliver what I think I need. I will say I love you one day, yet lash out at you in anger on another because somehow you have gotten in the way of my plan. What looks like God-contoured living is often, upon closer inspection, a shrink-wrapped existence.

Yet, it was never supposed to be this way. From the first moment of the creation of Adam and Eve, people were designed to live within the huge contours of the glory of God. We were not designed to settle for personal survival, temporal happiness, or individual success. We were created to find our meaning, identity, and purpose in the existence, character, and plan of God. Our identity was meant to be rooted in his love. Our hope was designed to be tied to his grace. Our potential was meant to be connected to his power. Our purpose was meant to be structured by his will. Our joy was meant to be wed to his glory. In every way, our vision of what is necessary, true, worthy, and meaningful was meant to be rooted in a functional worship of him. We were created for the dignity of living large and meaningful lives—lives that literally are connected to things before the creation of the world and extending far into eternity.

This results in an expansive existence, a kind of living that spans far beyond the normal things that would grip, engage, entertain, and fulfill the average human being. This kind of big-God, big-picture living means that we care about many things that do not actually touch or immediately involve us. And why do we care about these things? Because God, who is the source and center of our lives, does. God-contoured living means that God's purposes become our functional life goals, that things God says are valuable become the real-life treasures we seek, and that God's will provides the fences within which we live. The "more" we live for is his plan for us and for all things. We begin to get excited because we see how grace has connected our story to his sweeping story. We start to understand that grace cuts a hole in sin's shrink wrap. Grace reaches in, pulls us out, and locates us in a place that is more exciting and meaningful than anything we could have ever conceived of ourselves. This place is oxygenated by his love, invigorated by his power, and decorated with his glory. This huge and wonderful place, where we were meant to live and find our identity and purpose, is the kingdom of God.

THE CONTOURS OF THE SHRUNKEN KINGDOM

But, sadly, we all tend to get excited about another kingdom. Sin kidnaps our concern and atrophies our care. Sin blinds us to God's glory and leaves us deaf to his call. Tragically, sin leaves us all too willing to be satisfied with expending our gifts and energies on ourselves. Sin shrinks each of us to a mini-king, ruling our mini-kingdoms of one. It reduces the human community to a society of kings colliding with each other's solitary kingdoms. No wonder we live with such conflict in our individual lives and so much war in the global community! It is an act of God's grace that we can live with each other at all.

Maybe you're thinking at this point, "Okay, Paul, I get it. I understand the *shrink dynamic*, but I'm not sure I get what it looks like in the context of everyday living." So let's examine the narrow contours of the kingdom of self.

Here and now. The shrink-wrapped kingdom of self tends to have its eyes firmly focused on the present. It is about what I see, hear, think, and feel in the here and now. This kingdom isn't a kingdom of delayed gratification or persevering patience. It is an impatient kingdom that wants what it wants and wants it now.

But since we have immortal souls, we are designed to live with eternity always in view. This moment is but an introduction to, and a preparation for, what is to come. The entire length of our lives on earth is but an infinitesimal blip in time when compared with the expansiveness of the eternity that lies ahead of us. The culture of the big kingdom is shaped by eyes that are on eternity. The culture of the big kingdom sees *now* as an investment in *then*. The culture of the big kingdom finds value and joy in eternal investments, rather than in the endless catalog of temporary investments in the material joys of the here and now.

No, it is not evil to invest in a good car, to buy a good house, to enjoy a relaxing vacation, or to relish the pleasures of a succulent steak. Each of these things points, in some way, to the creative glory of God. The issue here is what drives the system. It is all about what you are living for, what gives you meaning and purpose, what gets you up in the morning, what gives you identity, where you seek to find joy, what you seek to satisfy your heart, and where you are looking to find life.

The kingdom of self tends to have its focus on the joys, pleasure, and pursuits of the here and now. No one critiques this way of living better than C.S. Lewis in *Mere Christianity*.

> If you read history, you will find that the Christians who did most for the present world were those who thought most of the next. The Apostles themselves, who set on foot the conversion of the Roman Empire, the great men who built up the Middle Ages, the English who abolished the Slave Trade, all left their mark on Earth, precisely because their minds were occupied with heaven. It is since Christians have largely ceased to think of the other world that they have become so ineffective in this one. Aim at

Heaven and you will get earth 'thrown in': aim at earth and you will get neither.[1]

Me and mine. The shrunken kingdom is also nearsighted. It doesn't see well at a distance. Its vision of what is needful, important, valuable, vital, urgent, worthwhile, and necessary tends to travel no further than the cares and concerns of self. Of course, I am supposed to be a good steward of the gifts the Lord has given me, and I should care for my immediate friends and family. It is not wrong to do so. What is wrong is to spend so much time caring for me that there is no time or energy left to expend on the cares and concerns of the vast universe that exist outside the borders of my life.

Perhaps something that happened to me in seminary would help illustrate this idea. I attended a seminary in Philadelphia that was located in an urban community scarred with all of the physical, personal, and socioeconomic blight that has inflicted many communities in America's greatest cities. Each day I would carpool to the seminary with three or four future pastors to study the rich theology of God's Word for the purpose of preparing ourselves to minister to sinners dealing with the difficulties of life in a broken world. We would have the most amazing and exciting conversations as we rode back and forth together. I loved those trips as much as I enjoyed the classes.

One morning the car was quiet, and I looked out the window beyond myself and my posse of future theologians. For the first time I really saw broken houses, cars, and people. There was crying need everywhere I looked. I sat in the back seat of that seminary-bound car and began to weep, not just at the obvious destructiveness of sin on that community, but at my own blindness. I had been in that community day after day, but I had been utterly blind to anything beyond me and mine. I was preparing for the ministry, but I had a shockingly uncaring heart.

Wants and needs. We all live with a sense of personal need and desire. It would be an act of irrationality to act as if you needed nothing. It is not wrong to desire certain things. Once more, the issue is what dominates your heart and sets the agenda for your life. Is so much of your time expended on caring for your own needs and satisfying your personal desires that you have little or no time left for the larger concerns of the kingdom of God?

The kingdom of self is fundamentally driven by a personal commitment to make sure I get everything I think I need and to do all I can to satisfy my every desire. It is not a kingdom that is shaped by what God wants and by what others need. My needs occupy so much space that it is hard for anything else to compete for my attention, energy, and interest.

Physical and material. The shrink-wrapped kingdom tends to be about what can be seen, heard, felt, touched, tasted, or in some way physically experienced. It is a lifestyle that is dominated by the physical experiences and pleasures of the physical creation. It is dominated by physical appearance and sensory pleasures.

Now, balance is needed here once again. We *are* physical people, and we *do* live in a beautifully created physical world. God has given us much to please our eyes and fill our stomachs. There are amazing pleasures to be enjoyed in the physical world, and it can be an act of worship to do so, but the danger is that life would be defined by things seen rather than things unseen. The kingdom of self tends to be more focused on what the hands can touch than what the heart should embrace.

Entitlements and rights. The kingdom of self tends to be a "this is what I deserve," "this is my position," "this is what belongs to me," and "this is how you should treat me" kingdom. It is a kingdom that finds greater delight in being served than in serving. Here you tend to be most grieved by offenses against yourself. Here you have a vigilant eye to how others are treating you. Here your relationships are shaped by your expectations for how the people around you should relate to you. Here you are very clear about your property, your position, and your rights.

Now, this does not mean it is godly to be a doormat or to willingly open yourself up for mistreatment or abuse. The issue again is what is driving the system. Is my life expended by a protection of personal boundaries, personal property, and personal entitlements; or am I willing to lay down my rights, to sacrifice my comfort, and even expose myself to mistreatment for the sake of the work of God's kingdom?

Sin holds the physical glories of the here-and-now world in front of you and tells you that they are the only glories worth living for. Sin shrinks your zeal and narrows your vision. Sin makes it hard to see beyond the borders of your own life. Grace enables you to tear down fences of self-focus, self-defensiveness, and self-protection so you can reach out to God and others. In so doing you will not only experience true glory, but you will recapture your true humanity.

THE FINAL QUESTION: HAS THE ENERGY OF YOUR LIFE BEEN EXPENDED IN THE NARROW WORLD OF PERSONAL WANTS, NEEDS, AND CONCERNS?

WHAT SITS SMACK-DAB IN THE
CENTER OF YOUR LIFE?

CHAPTER EIGHT

IN THE CENTER OF IT ALL

pre·em·i·nent: superior to or notable above all others, greatest in importance

THE BOTTOM LINE: BIG KINGDOM LIVING MEANS LIVING WITH CHRIST AT THE CENTER OF EVERYTHING I THINK, DESIRE, SAY, AND DO.

He just had to be the center of attention. No matter where they were or what they were doing, he seemed unable to be quiet and stay in the background. He got agitated when forced to share the stage with others and did everything he could to steal the spotlight. He was not interested in sharing, and he found no delight in serving. He did not like to obey, and he always thought that his way was the best way. He saw people as obstacles and circumstances outside of his control as dangerous. He demanded the attention of others and loudly protested when he did not get it. The problem was, not only was he obsessed with being at the center of it all, he was only eight years old!

I sat in my office with his exhausted, fearful, and discouraged parents. They were simply at the end of their rope. They had done everything they knew, and nothing seemed to make a difference. They dreaded the long nights at home, they feared taking him into public, and they were encountering all kinds of problems at school. He was the little lord of his universe, and he had done a good job of whipping his parents and others into shape.

As I sat with his parents and watched the dynamics of his relationship to them, there was one thing that kept coming into my mind. In the self-centeredness of this strong-willed little boy, I was looking at an example of what sin does to all of us. Sin causes all of us to want to live at the center of our worlds. Sin causes all of us to want the spotlight on ourselves. Sin causes all of us to focus our energies on our earth-bound treasures and anxiety-bound needs. Yes, sin really does cause all of us to shrink the size of our lives to the size of our lives. This *is* what the little kingdom is about. In the little kingdom, self is always at the center. In the big kingdom, the kingdom of God, the center is the one place self can never be. The fundamental difference between the two kingdoms can be seen in who resides in the center. Transcendent, big kingdom living always has the center reserved for someone other than you. This chapter is all about that Someone.

THE BIBLE: THE STORY OF THE KING

As we have said, the Bible is the story of a battle between the two kingdoms—the kingdom of self and the kingdom of God. But even more than that, the Bible is the story of the King. The bright and shining hope of the Old Testament, as it chronicles the failed kingdoms of man, is that a King was coming who would establish his kingdom and reign in justice and righteousness forever. (See Isaiah 9:6–9, Isaiah 32, Ezekiel 37:24ff, Zechariah 9:9–13.) The Old Testament calls the people of God to shift their hope from the flawed rule of human kings to the promise of One who would rule without sin forever. The Old Testament is a detailed history of how God accomplished all the necessary steps leading to the coming of the Promised King. At the same time it chronicles the irresistible tendency that sinners have to opt for self-rule, even in the face of the promise of this benevolent King. The Old Testament ends with God's people waiting, looking, and hoping for the King.

The Gospels announce the coming of the King and the establishment of his kingdom. This is the backdrop of every teaching of Christ, every miracle, and every provision. The long-awaited time had come. The feet of the King had touched the sod of earth. Matthew has an announcement or description of the kingdom in every chapter. The Epistles detail the glorious hope that sinners find in the Savior-King's rule of grace. In a real way, the entire Bible is the story of Christ the King. He *is* the One who alone is worthy of standing at the center of the kingdom of God. The big kingdom *is* the kingdom of Christ.

What this means practically is that *to live for the big kingdom is to live for Christ.* Transcendent living *is* Christ-centered living. Living for Christ is the only way you will ever be liberated from your bondage to the overwhelming tendency to shrink the size of your life to the size of your life. The only way to spin free of the narrow confines of your little cubicle kingdom is to live in the big sky country of Christ-centered living. You will never win the battle with yourself simply by saying "no" to yourself. That battle only begins to be won when you say "yes" to the call of your King, the Lord Jesus Christ.

PREEMINENT IN ALL THINGS

What does it mean to live in an intentionally Christ-centered way in your daily life—in your marriage, parenting, friendship, work, community, finances, etc.? Remember that only when you live for Christ can you recapture the transcendence for which you were created. Only in transcendent living can you recover your true humanity. And only in recovering your true humanity can your life really have meaning and purpose. All of this is true because your humanity is not tied to self-discovery and self-fulfillment (as the surrounding world proposes) but in investing your life for Christ's glory and the success of his kingdom on earth. You were put here for the purpose of the glory of another. This is not a lifestyle option; it is in the very nature of your humanity. To live for yourself is to rob yourself of your own humanity. It is only in living for Christ that we actually begin to become what we were meant to be.

Let me state it again. To live for the big kingdom is to live every dimension of my life in a Christ-centered way. Let's consider two passages from the Apostle Paul that focus on this truth. These passages are so foundational that I have included the full text of both. Let's look first at Colossians 1:3–23.

> We always thank God, the Father of our Lord Jesus Christ, when we pray for you, because we have heard of your faith in Christ Jesus and of the love you have for all the saints—the faith and love that spring from the hope that is stored up for you in heaven and that you have already heard about in the word of truth, the gospel that has come to you. All over the world this gospel is bearing fruit and growing, just as it has been doing among you since the day you heard it and understood God's grace in all its truth. You learned it from Epaphras, our dear fellow servant, who is a faithful minister of Christ on our behalf, and who also told us of your love in the Spirit.
>
> For this reason, since the day we heard about you, we have not stopped praying for you and asking God to fill you with the knowledge of his will through all spiritual wisdom and understanding. And we pray this in order that you may live a life

worthy of the Lord and may please him in every way: bearing fruit in every good work, growing in the knowledge of God, being strengthened with all power according to his glorious might so that you may have great endurance and patience, and joyfully giving thanks to the Father, who has qualified you to share in the inheritance of the saints in the kingdom of light. For he has rescued us from the dominion of darkness and brought us into the kingdom of the Son he loves, in whom we have redemption, the forgiveness of sins.

He is the image of the invisible God, the firstborn over all creation. For by him all things were created: things in heaven and on earth, visible and invisible, whether thrones or powers or rulers or authorities; all things were created by him and for him. He is before all things, and in him all things hold together. And he is the head of the body, the church; he is the beginning and the firstborn from among the dead, so that in everything he might have the supremacy. For God was pleased to have all his fullness dwell in him, and through him to reconcile to himself all things, whether things on earth or things in heaven, by making peace through his blood, shed on the cross.

Once you were alienated from God and were enemies in your minds because of your evil behavior. But now he has reconciled you by Christ's physical body through death to present you holy in his sight, without blemish and free from accusation— if you continue in your faith, established and firm, not moved from the hope held out in the gospel. This is the gospel that you heard and that has been proclaimed to every creature under heaven, and of which I, Paul, have become a servant.

In this prayer/hymn, Paul says it all. Christ is your hope. Christ is your wisdom. Christ is your strength. Christ is your rescue. Christ is your reconciliation. You have been called to a daily lifestyle where this Christ is preeminent in everything that makes up your life.

Or consider 1 Corinthians 1:18–2:5.

> For the message of the cross is foolishness to those who are
> perishing, but to us who are being saved it is the power of God. For
> it is written:
>> "I will destroy the wisdom of the wise;
>> the intelligence of the intelligent I will frustrate."
> Where is the wise man? Where is the scholar? Where is
> the philosopher of this age? Has not God made foolish the
> wisdom of the world? For since in the wisdom of God the
> world through its wisdom did not know him, God was pleased
> through the foolishness of what was preached to save those
> who believe. Jews demand miraculous signs and Greeks look
> for wisdom, but we preach Christ crucified: a stumbling block
> to Jews and foolishness to Gentiles, but to those whom God
> has called, both Jews and Greeks, Christ the power of God
> and the wisdom of God. For the foolishness of God is wiser
> than man's wisdom, and the weakness of God is stronger than
> man's strength.
>
> Brothers, think of what you were when you were called.
> Not many of you were wise by human standards; not many were
> influential; not many were of noble birth. But God chose the
> foolish things of the world to shame the wise; God chose the
> weak things of the world to shame the strong. He chose the lowly
> things of this world and the despised things—and the things that
> are not—to nullify the things that are, so that no one may boast
> before him. It is because of him that you are in Christ Jesus, who
> has become for us wisdom from God—that is, our righteousness,

holiness and redemption. Therefore, as it is written: "Let him who boasts boast in the Lord."

When I came to you, brothers, I did not come with eloquence or superior wisdom as I proclaimed to you the testimony about God. For I resolved to know nothing while I was with you except Jesus Christ and him crucified. I came to you in weakness and fear, and with much trembling. My message and my preaching were not with wise and persuasive words, but with a demonstration of the Spirit's power, so that your faith might not rest on men's wisdom, but on God's power.

What did Paul tell the Corinthian believers was the one irreducible element of his ministry? The centrality of the crucified Christ! Kingdom living, for Paul, puts Christ and his cross central in everything in the Christian's life. Having made brief comments about both of these passages, let me summarize them with the following principles.

The created world was designed to have Christ at the center. Romans 11:36 says it well: "For from him and through him and to him are all things. To him be the glory forever! Amen." Take this principle to every arena of your life. Your marriage has come from Christ, your marriage is to be lived unto Christ, and your marriage exists because of the grace of Christ. Your children are from your Lord, your children belong to him, and your children will only be what they were meant to be through his love and grace. Your possessions are from his hand, your possessions belong to him for his purpose, and your possessions will be kept by means of his care. There is nothing in your life that does not belong to Christ.

People were designed to live Christ-focused lives. True humanity is never to be found in autonomy, because human beings were wired to live in necessary community with the Creator. So anytime I functionally live for myself, I am denying the things for which I was made and opening my life to the negative fruit which will result. From day one, Christ was meant to be the focus of the life of everyone he created. That is the paradigm of the garden.

Christ-centered living is foolishness to the world. To most of the world, religion is the luxury of the strong and the sad necessity of the weak, but it is utter foolishness to structure your life around the purposes of a being that can neither be seen nor heard. The human ideal of Western culture is the self-made man. We honor the person who has made himself and who rules himself. From this perspective, it only makes sense that our own minds should be the court of highest judgment, and that pleasure should be our highest goal. It seems wise to deify the creation and to ignore the Creator. In this economy, this life is our focus and eternity simply doesn't exist. It is then the height of foolishness to think that my life would exist for the glory of another.

Focus on Christ will always result in focus on the cross. You cannot be Christ-centered without becoming cross-centered. The crucified Christ is to be the center of everything I know about myself and my world. You cannot have any real hope for flawed people in a fallen world unless there is a Redeemer to rescue us from the evil that resides both inside and outside of us. Real restoration to God's created design requires the cross. It is the cross of Christ that alone will restore my allegiance to Christ and his rightful place at the center of everything in my life.

SO WHAT DOES IT LOOK LIKE FOR CHRIST TO BE CENTRAL?

Sam was a Christian, but his faith lacked zeal and direction. He did all the right things, but they seemed empty and without energy. At work, however, he took on a completely different personality. He was positive, driven, interactive, and zealous. He arrived early to get a jump on his day, not because he was forced to but because he wanted to. Often he was the last person to head for home. In his walk with the Lord and his life with his church, he appeared neither excited nor engaged. Yet at work he was alive, every pore opened. Why the contrast? What *was* missing?

Here's what happens. When Christ isn't central in the life of a Christian, his Christianity will always get reduced to *theology* and *rules*. It will cease to be the central organizing principle of his life. It will give way to other powerful motivations and move to the fringes of his life. I think this is the experience of many Christians. Their Christianity is missing Christ! It then becomes little more than an ideology with an accompanying set of ethics. What is incredibly dangerous about this is that if Christ isn't central in our hearts, something else will be. Christianity as theology and rules will allow self to be at the center. It is only Christ who can free you and me from bondage to the little kingdom. Functionally, Sam's faith had been reduced to beliefs and commands. But Christianity gutted of Christ is devoid of both its beauty and its power. Only love for Christ has the power to incapacitate the sturdy love for self that is the bane of every sinner, and only the grace of Christ has the power to produce that love.

Yes, it is possible for Christ to be replaced, even in Christianity! It is possible for the little kingdom to look just like the big kingdom. *Christian activism,* a commitment to and enthusiasm for moral causes, can masquerade as a love for Christ. *Legalism* will masquerade as love for Christ with its rigid attention to law and its confidence in human righteousness. *Formalism* will wear the mask of love for Christ with its dedicated commitment to participation in all the scheduled gatherings and ministries of the church. *Emotionalism* with its powerful moments of heartfelt emotion will present itself as love for Christ. *Creedalism* with its strong allegiance to the purity of truth will seem like love for Christ. *Externalism* with its zeal to participate in all the outward signs of true Christian piety will look like love for Christ.

All of these things have a place in the big kingdom. All of them can be elements of love for Christ. But the danger of each is that they have the power to masquerade as love for Christ, effectively replacing him in our hearts. A person is fully able to pursue his little kingdom purposes and simultaneously think that he is living a Christ-centered life, when, in fact, his heart is ruled by neither the comfort of Christ's grace nor the call to love him above all else. There really is no place for Christ in many people's Christianity. Their faith is not actually in *Christ;* it is in *Christianity* and their own ability to live it out. This kind of "Christianity" is really about the shadow glories of human knowledge and performance. It does not require the death of self that must always happen if love for Christ is going to reign in our hearts.

So, what *does* big kingdom, Christ-centered living look like? This is what the rest of this book will be about. I want you to put down this book with a clear sense of what big kingdom, Christ-centered, transcendent living looks like in your everyday situations and relationships. Let me start by offering four words. In the next chapter we will look at a passage that will give us more concrete direction for living a Christ-centered life that really does make a difference in this fallen world. To live in a Christ-centered way means that Christ is my source, motive, goal, and hope.

Source. Here I am recognizing that everything that is really worth having is a gift from his hands. Here I recognize that I could not have written my own story. My location, gifts, talents, abilities, opportunities, and blessings all come from him. Here I also admit that I cannot be what I am supposed to be or do what I am supposed to do apart from a constant and continuing supply of his grace. I need wisdom, strength, love, patience, perseverance, and faith that I do not have on my own. To see Christ as your source means to measure your potential not by the limits of your natural ability, but by the unending resources of his grace. And since I am constantly dependent on his grace, I seek his grace wherever it is to be found. I read his Word, I fellowship with other believers, I participate in corporate worship, I am active in ministry, I participate in the Lord's Supper, and I seek the wise counsel of spiritual leaders. I do all of these things not out of duty, but because Christ is my source and I am a seeker after his grace.

Motive. To live a Christ-centered life means that he really is the reason

I do everything I do. I want to know him. I want to be part of his work on earth. I want to please him with my life. I want to value what he values. I want his purpose for me to define my purpose for myself. I want to follow his words and incarnate his character. I want to be his disciple and represent him like an ambassador so his will shapes my actions, reactions, words, thoughts, and desires. My decisions are more about what pleases him than what pleasures me. I am enthused that I have been selected to be part of his big kingdom, and I want to live in a way that fits with the goals, values, and purposes of it.

Goal. Living a Christ-centered life means that I willingly submit every other attainable glory in my life to the one glory that has captured my heart and structures my life, the glory of Jesus Christ. I do want him to be known, honored, worshipped, and obeyed. I do want his purposes to succeed. And although there are things that I would like to experience and accomplish, there is one orienting compass in my life. It is his honor and glory that I live for. I no longer live, decide, act, and relate for the purposes of my own glory. No, I have found something way more wonderful and beautiful, and he is what gives my life direction and joy.

Hope. What are you hoping for? What basket have you put all of your eggs in? Where do you tend to say, "If only I had _____, then my life would be great"? What do you look forward to and hope that you can experience? What occupies your mind and controls your dreams? Are you constantly investing in what can't deliver and won't last? Is Christ your hope? Is he the solid rock on which your life stands? When Christ is my hope, he becomes the one thing in which I have confidence. I act on his wisdom and I bank on his grace. I trust his promises and I rely on his presence. And I pursue all the good things that he has promised me simply because I trust him. So, I am not manipulating, controlling, or threatening my way through life to get what I want, because I have found what I want in Christ. He is my hope.

Consider these questions: What kingdom are you actually living for?

What is the "good life" that you daily pursue? What hope gets you up in the morning and keeps you going throughout the day? Is Christ the center of your life? If I watched the video of your last month, listening to what you said and why you said it, what would I notice most? If I watched how you made decisions and related to others, noting what you were interested in and fought for, what kingdom would it reveal? If I saw how you dealt with responsibility and invested your free time, and if I saw you in both busy and quiet moments, even hearing your silent conversations with yourself, would I conclude that Christ is the center of your life? Is he really your source, your motive, your goal, and your hope? Is it possible that your Christianity may, in fact, exclude Christ? Is it maybe possible that the little kingdom is alive and well, smack-dab in the middle of the big kingdom?

THE FINAL QUESTION: WHAT TENDS TO COMPETE WITH CHRIST FOR THE CENTER OF YOUR WORLD?

ARE YOU READY TO PARTICIPATE
IN YOUR OWN DEATH?

CHAPTER NINE

WELCOME TO YOUR DEATH

*dis·ci·ple: one who adheres to the teaching of another
and imitates his example*

THE BOTTOM LINE: IN CALLING US TO DIE, CHRIST IS ACTUALLY RESCUING US FROM DEATH AND GIVING US REAL LIFE.

We had avoided going into that room as long as we could. We knew it would not be comfortable, natural, or easy. We were sure none of us would leave the room with any joy. It would have been nice to have been able to talk about life, about tomorrow, about the future. But we went into the room that day to talk about death. Mom's body simply couldn't sustain her any longer. She was artificially kept alive by medical technology, and the doctor was there to ask us how long we wanted to keep her in that state. I remember thinking how universal the hatred of death is, how much grief was in this critical care unit, and how many people walking the halls were wishing that they could take life in their hands and give it back to a dying loved one.

In light of all this, it must have been a shock when Christ turned to his followers and announced that they must die. It was not much of a way to excite the crowd or market his kingdom! Christ was calling his listeners to something that is simply counterintuitive for us all. We all work to preserve both our physical lives and our own personal definition of life. We work hard to avoid danger, injury, suffering, difficulty, trial, and loss. This instinct to preserve and defend life is deep within all of us. Yet here the Creator of life is actually calling us to think positively about dying. It doesn't seem to make any sense. That is, until you begin to understand the profound logic in Christ's call.

Let's consider his words found in Luke 9:23–26.

> If anyone would come after me, he must deny himself and take
> up his cross daily and follow me. For whoever wants to save
> his life will lose it, but whoever loses his life for me will save
> it. What good is it for a man to gain the whole world, and yet
> lose or forfeit his very self? If anyone is ashamed of me and my
> words, the Son of Man will be ashamed of him when he comes
> in his glory and in the glory of the Father and of the holy
> angels.

Here is one of the most practical truths you will ever consider. It has everything to do with how you are presently investing your life, where you are placing your hope, and the transcendent life that you were created to enjoy. The little kingdom promises life, but brings you death; the big kingdom requires your death, but gives you life.

But you must remember that you will be continually tempted to think that the opposite is true. Let me say it even more forcefully. The biggest danger this side of eternity is *death pretending to be life*. Death pretended to be life in the garden and has been doing it ever since. Proverbs 14:12 summarizes death's trickery well: "There is a way that seems right to a man, but in the end it leads to death."

We sinners are very good at getting death and life confused. If you pay attention, you will see it all around you. Watch television, for example, where adultery is portrayed as life. Of course, a moment of sexual lust or even the act of illicit sex will seem invigorating at first. It may feel like life at its fullest. But adultery is a cruel investment of both the body and the soul. Scripture warns us where a relationship with an adulteress is heading: "In the end she is bitter as gall, sharp as a double-edge sword. Her feet go down to death; her steps lead straight to the grave" (Proverbs 5:4–5).

Or consider gluttony, which seems like a harmless enjoyment of the good things that the Lord created. It may feel like the good life, but it is actually robbing you of true life and destroying both your body and your soul. Material possessions are sold to us as if they have the power to give life. And because they can be seen and touched, they will seem like life. Surround yourself with fine things that indulge the senses, and you will experience very powerful sensual delights. But materialism actually robs you, because the material things that rule your heart cannot give you life. Materialism will atrophy your soul and end in death.

Again and again the Bible warns us that life consists in more than physical "bread." You see the trickery functioning even in children. To a child, getting his own way and parenting himself will seem like real life. Disobedience will seem like a quicker path to the good life than obedience. But the Bible says just the opposite. Long life is the promise to those who honor and obey their parents.

So we need to hear the warning of Christ, because the "death pretending to be life" trick will be played on each of us again and again. I want to organize what Christ said in Luke under four headings—*the call, the logic, the question,* and *the warning.* Let's examine Christ's words together.

THE CALL: YOU MUST DIE

Jesus said, "If you want to be part of me and my kingdom, you must *deny yourself, take up your cross, and follow me*" (author's emphasis). This call to a three-fold death is the only door to a life that is really life. Jesus calls each of his disciples to follow his example. He who died to give us life promises life to those who are willing to die.

Deny yourself: death to the priority of self. From the earliest age, our love of self shapes everything we do and say. We fight over toys, the last bowl of cereal, and who gets the bathroom first. We work to be thought of as right, to be viewed as attractive, to win the argument with a neighbor, to get the promotion. We strive to be first, best, the center, the most powerful, the best known, the most loved. We really do love us and have a wonderful plan for our own lives! We indulge our desires and do anything we can to meet our own "needs." If we were really honest, many of us would say that we would be completely satisfied living our own lives for the sake of our own selves. But Christ asks us to do something unthinkable. He asks us to be willing to say "no" to the one person we have the most trouble saying no to—us!

Essentially Christ is saying, "If you want to live, if you want to experience the transcendent joys of my eternal kingdom, then you must let go of your hold on your life. You must loosen your grip and with open hands give your life back to me." Now ask yourself: "Am I following Christ's call where I live and work?" Perhaps you're thinking, *Frankly, Paul, I'm not sure what that would look like.* Well, think of your life as an investment. Every day each of us invests our time, money, gifts, talents, energies, relationships, and resources in the pursuit of something. Is your life invested in pursuing your life? Does it have a higher goal than your personal wants and needs? Do you find it hard to say "no" to you? Do you find yourself struggling with irritation, impatience, and anger when others unwittingly get in the way of what you want? Are you still holding tightly onto your life as if it really did belong to you?

Take up your cross: death to my pursuit of my life. The cross sticks out in Scripture. It seems crazy, like the greatest aberrant moment of all of history. It seems like a big mistake, a very bad joke. Surely nothing good could come out of God taking on human life and then being publicly, viciously, and unjustly mutilated. There were no positive connotations to the cross. It was the most horrible punishment reserved for the lowliest and vilest of criminals. It was a public shame on a hill outside of the city, and it always ended in death.

Yet the cross is not a bad joke. It is history's most beautiful paradox. The death of the Messiah was the only way he could give life to those who would believe in him. The hope of the cross is in its willing sacrifice of One for the sake of another. This is exactly what Christ's call to daily take up your cross is about. The one who sacrificed his life so that we might have life now calls his disciples to sacrifice their lives for him. In a world that only understands the kingdom of self, living for the big kingdom of Christ will always require suffering and sacrifice.

What are you unwilling to offer? Your money? Your lifestyle? Your reputation? Your house? Prestige? Power? The esteem of others? Your car? Your friendships? Your plans for the future? Which of these pleasures would you refuse to nail to your daily cross?

Follow me: death to my pursuit of my plan. Where are you going with your life? Whose plan are you following? Whose dream shapes the decisions that you make and the actions that you take? Who sets the agenda for a given day, week, month, or year? If you could accomplish your plan, what would your life look like? Here Christ calls us to the death of self-rule. He calls us to submit all that we do to his purpose for our lives. As his children, no longer are we to live as little self-lords, exercising sovereignty over our own lives. No, we are called to something bigger than anything we would plan for ourselves. Everything we think, desire, say, and do must fit within the new identity that we have been given. We have been chosen and called to be *followers*. That means we no longer live with a *master* mentality. We have been bought and paid for by his blood, and our lives no longer belong to us. (See 1 Corinthians 6:19–20.) Which identity shapes your actions, reactions, and responses to life? Do you walk through your life like a mini-king? Do you try to squeeze the call of Christ into the contours of your self-designed master plan?

Bill had conceived his master plan when he was still in high school. He knew just what he wanted to be and exactly what he wanted his life to look like. He was determined that no obstacle would trip him up. The problem was that Bill was a committed believer, and his plan had begun to collide with God's plan for him. His plan left little time for investment in his family and his church. His plan left few resources to serve others. His plan was *his* plan, and it was so tightly woven that there was no place to squeeze God into it. Bill never forsook his faith or left his church, but at a deep personal level there was little that was Christian about his living. Bill's problem was that Bill was Bill's master. He had never taken on a follower's identity.

Christ calls each of his children to this three-fold death: death to the priority of self, death to our pursuit of our lives, and death to our pursuit of our own plan. Are you living as his disciple in this way? Are you following his example? Only as we die to the glory of our claim on our own lives will we begin to experience the transcendent glories of living for the Lord. Only when we are willing to do the unthinkable (preside over our own deaths) does the wonderful (the transcendence for which we were created) become our possession.

THE LOGIC: RESCUE FROM SPIRITUAL SUICIDE

Why is the call of Christ so hard? Why will he settle for nothing less than this triple death? The answer is because Christ knows us. He knows the character and inertia of sin. Sin in its essence is self-focused. Sin pulls all of us away from the big kingdom and toward the little kingdom. Sin causes my heart to be ruled by personal desire and felt need. Sin makes me want to set my own rules for me and others. Sin will even cause me to co-opt the grace of God for the purposes of my own agenda. Sin makes me want to write my own story and to have God endorse it. Sin makes me demanding and impatient. Sin causes me to wrap both of my hands around my life and do anything I can to preserve it for my own purpose.

Christ, on the other hand, not only calls us to be willing participants in our own death, but he also lays out the logic behind his call. It is found in this one profound big kingdom principle: *Try to save your life and you will lose it, but lose your life for Christ's sake and you will find it.* Once again, the little kingdom promises you life but brings you death, while the big kingdom requires your death but gives you life. To jealously hold on to my dream of what I want to accomplish, experience, and enjoy is to guarantee that I will never ever experience true life. Instead, I will experience the slow and progressive shrinking of my soul until there is no life left. You see, our life cannot be found outside of our relationship to the Lord. So, if I am seeking life outside of the One who *is* life, I am effectively committing spiritual suicide.

The promises of the little kingdom will always fail. They will always leave me coming up short, because the spiritual oxygen that my heart needs to breathe can only be found in the Lord. Achievement, acceptance, appearance, and possessions may give you identity, meaning, and purpose for a while. But they will enslave you in the process and disappoint you in the end. There are more of us out there with these suicidal intentions than not. We are drinking from dry wells and breathing what is not oxygen, but we don't even know that we are dying in the process.

When you hold onto your life in order to guarantee that you will have life, you destroy any possibility of experiencing the life you were put on earth to enjoy. Those transcendent joys and pleasures for which you were created are only available to you on the other side of your death.

Let me give you one example. In Matthew 6:19–34, Christ teaches that living for my own provision and pleasure leads to worry and anxiety.

And worry never changes anything in my life. At the end of an hour of anxious fretting, none of the things that I have worried about have changed a bit. Yet worry changes me. It is a cancer on my soul. Worry eats away at my time, rest, strength, courage, hope, character, relationships, purpose, worship, joy, and satisfaction. I tell myself that worrying will protect my life, but what I am really experiencing is the death of many good things within me. Holding onto my life is a plan doomed to failure. It is a disease that is always terminal. It will never work.

Admit it, you love you and have a wonderful plan for your life. Your loving Lord knows it, too. He knows how sturdy and resilient your allegiance to your own life is. He knows the power of that personal desire to control, maintain, preserve, and rule your life. He knows this power is so strong that death is the only solution. Until you give up your life, you will always be tempted to substitute the real life of loving, obedient worship of the King for something else that is incapable of giving you life.

THE QUESTION: WHAT IF YOU HAD IT ALL?

I remember the scene so well. It was as if it was designed right from this passage. In the center was a gorgeous house, positioned high on a hill, with an entire wall made of glass. It was surrounded by carefully manicured grounds, with lush trees and beautiful flowers. I came to know each one of them because I was his gardener. There was the requisite swimming pool and a very large greenhouse. The garage was huge, but luxury automobiles lined the driveway. I could not think of anything this man did not have. He was fabulously wealthy. He had power and position. He had more possessions than he knew what to do with. The whole town woke up each morning under the looming shadow of his mansion. He had it all. But he was a soulless man!

Could there be anything sadder than for a man to live, work, and achieve, only to miss the one thing in life that is truly worth living for? The problem with the man on the hill was not his riches. The problem was that he lived for his riches, and so became shockingly spiritually poor. There is no investment as poor as investment in the kingdom of self! What good would it do to become the richest person on earth and yet miss the one thing that you were placed on earth to experience—that is, intimacy with God and commitment to his glory?

I know all of this, yet still a luxurious meal with my wife can seem more like life than giving that money to the work of God's kingdom. And the acceptance of a friend can appear more life-giving than the love of the Lord. The accumulation of possessions can seem functionally more life-giving than growth in character. It is so easy to invest your life in all the wrong kinds of treasure. It is so hard to remember that the most important things in life are things unseen. My employer on the hill had not invested his life well. Jesus would say there simply wasn't any profit in the way he had lived his life.

THE WARNING: THE DANGER OF PREFERRING THE LITTLE KINGDOM

In Luke 9:26, Jesus is basically saying, "Be ashamed of me, and I will be ashamed of you." What does he mean? To be ashamed of Jesus is to prefer the world and what it has to offer. It means to functionally deny Christ his rightful place in your life. It means to offer the rulership of the thoughts and desires of your heart to something other than Christ. It means to reject Christ's offer of life and seek to find life somewhere else. It means to elevate the value of the treasures of this present physical world above the surpassing value of knowing Christ.

Now understand, Christ is not talking about the theology you profess to believe, what you would write in a formal statement of faith. Rather, he is talking about what treasures or pleasures so excite and motivate you that they shape everything you desire, think, speak, and do. And here is the warning, "Deny me my rightful place in your life, and I will deny you a place with me in glory." It is a warning that we, with our quickly wandering hearts, should not take lightly.

Do you esteem Christ on Sunday yet invest the passion and action of your life in other treasures during the week? Yes, you must work, eat, rest, invest, and relate. The issue here is about what rules your heart and sets the agenda for your decisions and actions.

A SWEET PROMISE

The call of Christ *does* seem hard. "Deny yourself, take up your cross, and follow me." But this hard call is actually the call of grace. It is actually a means of rescue. In calling you to your death, Christ is actually protecting you *from* death. Your Lord knows that you have suicidal tendencies, so he will not leave you to yourself. He knows that you will tend to look at life and see death and look at death and see life. He knows that you will hold with clenched fists to what is not yours and refuse to open your hands to what is a gift. What could be more horrible than to get everything I want and miss the one thing that I was made for? His death call is really an offer to a life beyond your wildest dreams—a life of joy, satisfaction, purpose, and pleasure that this sadly broken world could never deliver in its finest moment. Shrinking your life to the size of your life is not life. It is death wearing the mask of life.

Yet, because of God's endless love and amazing grace, every one of his calls to us is wrapped in comfort. Each command is welcome, and each plea is dyed with mercy. Listen to the invitation recorded in Isaiah 55:1–2.

> Come, all you who are thirsty,
>   come to the waters;
> and you who have no money,
>   come, buy and eat!

Come, buy wine and milk
without money and without cost.
Why spend money on what is not bread,
and your labor on what does not satisfy?
Listen, listen to me, and eat what is good,
and your soul will delight in the richest of fare.

There is a rich and satisfying life to be found. There are delights to be known that will transcend anything you could plan or achieve for yourself. If you are God's child, your life has transcendent meaning and purpose. But these things will never be found as long as you are holding tightly to your life. Isaiah would say to each of us, "Why are you working so hard for what will never satisfy? Why are you investing so much in what can never fulfill?" This amazing life of transcendent meaning, purpose, and joy is to be found on the other side of your death. It is only when you deny yourself, take up your cross, and follow your Lord that you begin to experience the transcendent humanity for which you were created.

Remember, Christ's call to you is a rescue. In asking you to deny yourself and follow, he is giving to you what you could never earn or achieve on your own. You will not find it in your marriage, in parenting your children, in accumulating possessions, in the esteem of friends, in theological knowledge, or in the most beautiful location. Christ offers you what you cannot earn and what the physical creation can never offer: the all-surpassing glory of knowing him. This is the world's best prize. This is the universe's best meal. This is the only thing that will give your life meaning and fill you with lasting joy.

THE FINAL QUESTION: IN YOUR EVERYDAY SITUATIONS AND RELATIONSHIPS, WHERE ARE YOU FINDING IT HARD TO DENY YOURSELF, TAKE UP YOUR CROSS, AND FOLLOW CHRIST?

WHERE IS
YOUR FOCUS?

CHAPTER TEN

THE JESUS FOCUS

fo·cus: a central point, as of attraction, attention, or activity

THE BOTTOM LINE: AT STREET LEVEL, BIG KINGDOM LIVING IS JESUS-FOCUSED LIVING.

I thought it was a pretty hokey name for a ministry, but the concept behind the name grew on me. It was called "Jesus Focus Ministry." There is a way in which this name says it all. This is what we have been called to. By God's grace we have been rescued from me-focused living. Sin has given all of us a tendency to live in a way that is dictated by little more than earth-bound treasures and anxiety-bound needs. But grace calls us to live in a new and better way, a way that is focused on the person, the work, and the will of the Lord Jesus Christ. Grace punctures our self-contained little kingdoms and places us in the spaciousness of God's big kingdom. The big kingdom *is* the big kingdom *because* it has Jesus as the focus, Jesus at the center. When Jesus is no longer the focus and no longer at the center, the big kingdom splinters into a million little solitary kingdoms under the rulership of self. Big kingdom living *is* Jesus-focused living. But what exactly does this mean?

This is the question we have been considering in the last two chapters, but I want to hone our definition even more. My concern here is that we Christians tend to talk in a coded, quasi-biblical language that can cloud understanding as much as benefit it. I was once speaking at a retreat on the topic of the life of faith. I started out by asking the group to define faith for me. The first respondent said, "It means to believe." So, I said, "What does it mean to believe?" Someone called out, "It means to trust." So, I asked, "What does it mean to trust?" And the answer came back, "It means to have faith." Do you see what happened here? Coded biblical language was used to define coded biblical language. The terms were all familiar because they were constantly in use, not because they were well understood. In fact, as our discussion went further and deeper, it became clear that few in the room had a precise, functional definition of faith. Yet the apostle Paul said, "The just shall live by faith." What could be more basic to a believer than to understand the true nature of biblical faith?

So, I want to focus our definition of big kingdom, Christ-centered living even more. Big kingdom living is living with the purpose, character, call, grace, and glory of the Lord Jesus Christ as the central motivation and hope for everything you think, desire, do, and say. It is by living this way that you will once again experience the transcendence for which you were created and be freed from your bondage to you. And living this way will result in a life of meaning and purpose, where you really do make a difference wherever God places you.

JESUS-FOCUSED LIVING: A MODEL

There is a passage in the Old Testament that defines big kingdom, Christ-centered living more clearly than almost any other. Yes, it is possible to find a Christ-centered passage in the Old Testament, since Jesus is the Lord of the Old Testament as well as the New. This passage is found in the middle of God's final instructions to Israel as they were getting ready to cross the Jordan River into the land of promise. Whenever I read this portion of God's Word it feels like the kind of conversation parents would have with their child as they drop her off for her first year of college. Just before they drive away, they try to download into her brain a summary of all the important instructions and values that they have tried to inculcate into her over the last eighteen years. It is a whole-life biblical worldview, with all the necessary theology, ethics, and apologetics summarized in under five minutes! This passage is just that content rich.

> And now, O Israel, what does the LORD your God ask of you but to fear the LORD your God, to walk in all his ways, to love him, to serve the LORD your God with all your heart and with all your soul, and to observe the LORD's commands and decrees that I am giving you today for your own good?
>
> To the LORD your God belong the heavens, even the highest heavens, the earth and everything in it. Yet the LORD set his affection on your forefathers and loved them, and he chose you, their descendants, above all the nations, as it is today. Circumcise your hearts, therefore, and do not be stiff-necked any longer. For the LORD your God is God of gods and Lord of lords, the great God, mighty and awesome, who shows no partiality and accepts no bribes. He defends the cause of the fatherless and the widow, and loves the alien, giving him food and clothing. And you are to love those who are aliens, for you yourselves were aliens in Egypt. Fear the LORD your God and serve him. Hold fast to him and take your oaths in his name. He is your praise; he is your God, who performed for you those great and awesome wonders you saw with your own eyes. Your forefathers who went down into Egypt

were seventy in all, and now the LORD your God has made you
as numerous as the stars in the sky.

—DEUTERONOMY 10:12–22

THE BIG QUESTION

This passage begins with a great question, as good of a question as anyone who is committed to big kingdom living could ever ask: "What does God ask of you?" The issue here is not doing a bunch of *new and different* things, but responding to the things God has already placed in your life in a *very new* way. Consider a few examples. What does God ask of you as a husband or wife? What does God ask of you as a parent? What does God ask of you as a friend or neighbor? What does God ask of you as a member of the body of Christ? What does God ask of you as a citizen of your community, city, state, and nation? What does God ask of you as a worker or an employer? What does God ask of you as an inhabitant of the physical planet earth? What does God ask of you in regard to your possessions and finances? The way you answer these questions will powerfully shape the way you live your life.

Let's consider Deuteronomy's threefold answer to this vital question, captured by three profound words—*fear, act, love.*

Fear. What is this "fear of the LORD" about anyway? In our comfortable, meet-my-needs, God's-my-best-buddy form of Christianity, this is a very timely call. Fear of the Lord means that I carry around with me such a deep awareness, awe, and reverence for the power, holiness, wisdom, and grace of God that I would not think of doing anything other than living for his glory. Fearing the Lord means that this worshipful awe is the single and unchallenged motivator of everything I think, desire, say, and do.

What does it mean to live a Christ-centered existence? It means that the fear of the Lord, more than fear of anything else, sets the agenda for our actions, reactions, and responses. This is the essence of big kingdom living.

The kingdom of self is driven by all kinds of other fears: fear of man, fear of discomfort or difficulty, fear of failure, fear of not getting my own way, etc. The principle here is that if God doesn't own the fear of our hearts, he will not own our lives. You and I are always living to avoid what we dread. If we dread displeasing God more than anything else, because our hearts have been captured by a deep, worshipful and loving awe of him, we will live in new ways.

Act. Big kingdom, Christ-centered living is not just about an attitude of heart, but about a way of living as well. Living a God-centered life has not been left in a cloud of mystery for us. God has given us his Word as a functional guide for our everyday living. We do not need to be confused about what it means to be a God-centered neighbor, parent, spouse, friend, worker, or citizen. We do not need to fret over what it means to handle our possessions, finances, grief, anger, opportunities, and responsibilities in a godly way. We do not need to be confused about what we are to do with our thoughts, what should control our desires, or where we should place our hopes. God has precisely revealed his will for our daily living in his Word. Our principal job in life is not to uncover mystery. Our principal job is to obey what has already been revealed. Our job as we awake each morning is not to figure out how we would like to respond to what is on our plate. The commands, directives, and principles of God's Word are meant to guide us in how we live to serve him.

Love. The fundamental difference between big kingdom and little kingdom living is what has captured the love of our hearts. Remember, as Christ said during his earthly ministry, the kingdom of God is not a location. You couldn't say, "Honey, let's get up tomorrow morning and go visit the kingdom of God for the day." No, Jesus said, "The kingdom of God is within you." Both the big and little kingdoms are kingdoms of the heart. The big kingdom is shaped by a deeply thankful love for God, and the little kingdom is shaped by a love of self. When my true spiritual condition reveals that I, in fact, love me more than anything else, I will always shrink the size of my care and concern, sacrifice and discipline, and hopes and dreams to the size of my own life. If I love God more than anything else, I will be pulled way beyond the borders of my own wants and needs to the spaciousness of God's kingdom, where redemption and restoration of all things is the order of the day, every day. Big kingdom and little kingdom living are all about who or what owns your love.

When you are jealous of a fellow worker, what owns your love? When you are arguing with your wife, what owns your love? When you'll do anything to get someone's acceptance, who owns your love? When you are depressed because your plans have been thwarted, who owns your love? When you are numbing yourself with too much computer or too much television, who owns your love? When you give out of your own need, who owns your love? When you decide not to takes sides, but to be a peacemaker, who owns your love? When you resist vengeance and give mercy, who owns your love?

THE THING TO REMEMBER

In this model of Christ-centered living, the big question (What does God ask of me?) is followed by an important reminder: Big kingdom living is always propelled by remembering the Lord. Shockingly, he is the one thing that we sinners all tend to forget. Our thoughts can be so dominated by the necessary tasks of the day, by the difficulties we face, or by the people around us, that we lose our consciousness of the Lord of Glory who has drawn us into his transcendent purposes for the universe. Or our day can be kidnapped by anxious cravings and all the "what ifs" that worry is able to generate. Big kingdom living really does start with remembering the King. This isn't some mystical spiritual exercise for the super spiritual. It is street-level worship. It is loving God more than the projects on my PDA. It is caring more about his glory than about my schedule. It is caring that his grace is spread and his fame is known more than I care about the next sale, the next promotion, an immaculate house, or a fun lunch with my friends. Ask yourself, when you start your day, what fills the eyes of your heart? What "unseen" thing draws and motivates you? Do you see God? Are you drawn toward him? Do you desire that your day be his day? Do you recognize his grace, power, and sovereignty in your life?

Let's return to Deuteronomy 10. Verse 14 in the English Standard Version begins with the word, "Behold," which is just a formal way of saying, "Look!" Here is what the author is calling to your attention about the Lord.

1. Everything in heaven and earth belongs to him. This really is *his* world. I should never ever live as if it belongs to me.
2. You are who you are and what you are because of his grace. (Verse 15, ESV: "The LORD set his heart in love on your fathers.")
3. Your Lord is the most powerful Ruler of rulers. (Verse 17, ESV: "For the LORD your God is God of gods and Lord of lords, the great, the mighty, and the awesome God.")
4. He is the Lord of justice, love, and mercy. (Verses 18–19: "He defends the cause of the fatherless and the widow, and loves the alien, giving him food and clothing. And you are to love those who are aliens, for you yourselves were aliens in Egypt.")

What would a lifestyle of "seeing" the Lord look like? It would mean that everything that I have or could ever touch or experience did not belong to me for my use, but to the Lord for his use. It would mean walking through life not discontent because of all the things I don't have, but living with a deeply felt gratitude for all the things that I have but do not deserve. It would mean living with hope and courage, not because I have established my own base of power, but because I rest in the power of my Lord and the guaranteed success of everything he has promised. And it means that I will commit myself to more than personal survival, contentment, and happiness. No, like him, I will be committed to a life of justice, love, and mercy. I will not allow the size of my care and concern to atrophy to the size of my own life.

Remembering the Lord is an important discipline of big kingdom, Christ-centered living.

THE CALL

The big question and the reminder of Deuteronomy 10 are followed by a call to an attitude of heart. This is the bottom line. Remember, the war between the little kingdom and the big kingdom is essentially a war for the heart. The fear and love that rules your heart will shape your life. Isn't it encouraging that the bright promise of the work of Jesus is a new heart? Because Christ lived, died, and rose again, there is heart-transforming grace available to you. So, it makes perfect sense that this passage which calls us to forsake our little kingdom intentions would call us to a lifestyle-shaping condition of the heart.

THE FINAL QUESTION: WHAT IS THE FOCUS OF YOUR LIFE'S ENERGIES AND INTENTIONS?

WHAT MAKES YOU GROAN?

CHAPTER ELEVEN

GROANING

*sat·is·fac·tion: the confident acceptance of something
as satisfactory, right, dependable, or true*

THE BOTTOM LINE: THIS SIDE OF ETERNITY, THERE SHOULD BE DISSATISFACTION IN ALL OF US WITH THE WAY THINGS ARE.

As she stood on the porch and watched the kids waiting for the bus for the first day of school, it hit her: She had everything she had ever wanted. Three days earlier she and Brent had come home with the children from a wonderful week at the shore. The garden behind their 150-year-old farmhouse was laden with vegetables ready to be harvested. Brent had a great job, was a fairly skilled handyman around the house, and on top of all of that, was Kat's best friend. The single-block downtown in the small town where they lived was something out of a 1950's movie, and they lived only thirty miles from the big city where they could get anything they could ever want or need, and all of the art and culture they could ever want to enjoy.

Kat had a close circle of women friends, all of whom were approximately her age and who had young children like her own. She loved the Tuesday play date each week. While the kids romped in someone's yard, she and her friends would talk, laugh, and share for what seemed like hours. As she stood there and looked at Josh, Evan, and Cassie, they seemed like the perfect family.

The profit they had made from their well-located condo in the city had not only enabled them to buy the farmhouse of their dreams, but to completely restore the interior as well. The wraparound porch with its white wicker furniture had become an evening retreat whenever the weather was right. And she did love the garden. In the city she had barely been able to keep a couple of houseplants alive. Now they were actually eating vegetables that they had grown!

As the bus drove away, Kat, now lost in her thoughts, sat down on one of the wicker chairs. Her mind went to Brent. She remembered the night she met him; that is, if you can call bumping into someone and spilling your soda on them a meeting. She loved his sense of humor that night, so she agreed to see him again. Kat had recently had her heart broken and wasn't really interested in a relationship, but she agreed to go out with Brent because he made her laugh. Their relationship wasn't perfect, but Kat knew what some of her friends were going through in their marriages and she knew she had a lot to be thankful for. She smiled as she thought of Brent, standing in front of the mirror in his silly kangaroo boxers, shaving as fast as he could so he could throw on his clothes and head to his office in the city. She laughed as she anticipated that he would hit the porch soon, lukewarm coffee in hand, tie askew, already late as usual. As she quickly kissed Brent goodbye, she was thankful that he had found his niche and was experiencing real success in his job.

The call from the prayer chain made her mind go to the small-town church they had decided to make their own. The building, just off the town square, was something out of a postcard. Although the pastor wasn't the best communicator, he was very warm, and the church was so conveniently located for them. She had had fun organizing the nursery and painting and decorating the room that had new life each Sunday, as it was filled with the sound of infants and young mothers. Kat and Brent had never attended a church this small, but the family atmosphere had more than compensated for the lack of programs and activities that the big-city church had offered. She could see the steeple from her porch, and when the kids got older, they would probably join the town tradition of walking to church on Sunday.

Suddenly, Kat remembered that she had a lot to do before meeting Brent in the city for supper and a play. She grabbed her teacup and went inside to deal with the gotta-get-to-school-quickly mess that was always left in the children's wake as they ran out the door each morning. Even with a day of work in front of her, Kat thought about how much she loved her life.

TOO EASILY SATISFIED

It is right for Kat to be thankful for the good things that God has placed in her life, but there is something wrong with the way Kat responds to them that gets right at the heart of what big kingdom living is all about.

It is true that God created all the things that Kat now enjoys. They are direct gifts from his most gracious hands, and each of them is good in itself. To some extent it is even healthy for Kat to have reached a measure of fulfillment. But this is where the problem hides in this otherwise idyllic scene.

From a distance, Kat and Brent's life looks godly. They aren't overtly breaking any of God's commands. They have forged a fairly healthy relationship. They have involved themselves in their church. They seek to teach their children the things of the Lord. They're not in constant conflict or in deep debt. They have cordial relationships with their neighbors. Yet, there is something very wrong in this scene. Maybe what appears to be godly isn't so godly after all. Being ungodly is not just about committing a certain lists of sins. It is also about finding fulfillment outside of God, which leads me to commit an endless list of sins of the heart.

The problem with Kat is that she *is* so fulfilled. There is little evidence of discontent or dissatisfaction. And although she really is a Christian, there is little evidence that her contentment has anything at all to do with the kingdom of God. Kat is thrilled that her little kingdom dreams have almost all come true. The problem is that she seldom groans.

A TIME TO GROAN

It has been suggested by some that between coming to Christ and entering the final kingdom the default language of every Christian should be groaning. Paul says it this way in Romans 8:22–25.

> We know that the whole creation has been groaning as in the
> pains of childbirth right up to the present time. Not only so, but
> we ourselves, who have the firstfruits of the Spirit, groan inwardly
> as we wait eagerly for our adoption as sons, the redemption of our
> bodies. For in this hope we were saved. But hope that is seen is no
> hope at all. Who hopes for what he already has? But if we hope
> for what we do not yet have, we wait for it patiently.

Notice the logic of this passage. We are *supposed* to groan because there are things that we have been promised but do not yet have. We are supposed to groan because the full expression of God's kingdom has not yet come. We are supposed to groan because we are not yet all that God shed the blood of his Son for us to become. We are supposed to groan because the temporary pleasures of this physical world do not satisfy us; they always leave a void in our hearts. We are supposed to groan because in every situation and circumstance we see the damage that sin has done and is doing. We are supposed to groan because we recognize how we each give in to the temptation to seek in the physical world what we can only find in the Lord and what will only be fulfilled in eternity. This side of eternity, groaning is meant to be the default language of the big kingdom. When we groan for these reasons, we get it right. This kind of groaning is only present in people who are submitting little kingdom desires to big kingdom interests.

SHRINKAGE AND SATISFACTION

The problem with Kat is not that she is thankful. The problem is that she is too easily satisfied and in so doing, she has unwittingly shrunk the size of her life to the size of her life. Yes, she is committed to live as the Bible says to live, but inside the borders of this overtly committed Christian lifestyle, something significant is amiss. Redemptive groaning—the kind of painful cry of the children of God that is pictured in Romans 8—is completely absent in Kat's life. And the shocking thing is that when you scratch below the surface, Kat's satisfaction has nothing to do with the Lord. It simply isn't godly.

Let's examine Kat's satisfaction.

The temporary fulfillments of the physical, here-and-now world. What is the source of Kat's fulfillment? It is that she has been able to acquire and experience all the things she dreamed of in this physical world. She has the country cottage in the picturesque small town. She has a good-looking, nice, hardworking husband. She has three healthy children and a garden out back. She has all the art and culture she could ever want in the big city, only a half hour away. She has a fun circle of friends who are fairly easy to be around. Their bills are paid, and there is plenty of food in the pantry.

But these things were never meant to be the source of her personal fulfillment. Underneath the veneer of faith, Kat's satisfaction has little to do with God and what God wants for his world. It is all about what Kat wants and the fact that she has been able to get it. Right in the middle of the big kingdom that God has welcomed her into by his grace is little kingdom living. And if something would happen to Brent, if he lost his job and they had to sell the house, or if one of her children became sick, Kat's inner sense of joy and well-being would immediately disappear. Her satisfaction in these things is not godly because it is not God-ward. If you were to watch the video of Kat's life, you would see no sense that she is living for something bigger than herself. She is not looking expectantly for something she does not have. There is no sense of sadness that what God has begun still stands tragically incomplete. She doesn't act like someone in the pains of childbirth, in painful anticipation of what is to come. No, Kat is satisfied with the physical things that she has been able to collect in the here and now, and that is her problem.

The halfway-done work of redemption. On one hand, Kat is thankful that she is a Christian and is married to a Christian man. She is thankful for the things that she has come to believe and the principles that guide her life. But, here again, she is all too satisfied. Kat's video would not reveal a woman who is examining, striving, working, and praying to grow. Instead, she is completely satisfied with the work that God has begun in her, even though it is quite incomplete. Personal spiritual growth simply isn't high on Kat's agenda. Sure, she attends church and the women's Bible study. And yes, she is glad for her Christian husband, but there is little personal zeal to grow closer to the Lord in character and faith. Kat is content with the halfway-done work of redemption in her own life.

The same is true of Kat as she looks at the world around her. Sure, like others, she will complain about how rude people can be, about the corruption in politics, and about the problems of the inner city. She will occasionally shed a tear when she sees a report on starving children in Africa or the ravages of a recent storm. But she simply doesn't look at her world with big kingdom eyes. Kat doesn't groan for her world because she is pretty content with it. She doesn't fight much traffic, she has found a good grocery store, the mayor of her small town is her neighbor and a nice guy, and her property is big enough that she doesn't have to work very hard to get along with anybody. Kat doesn't weep inside for her world, because she looks at it with little kingdom eyes. Although her world is far from what the big kingdom says it could be, it serves Kat's little kingdom interests and so it is all basically okay with her. She knows almost nothing of the big kingdom groaning that is the default language of Romans 8.

Mutually satisfying, casual community. If you were to watch the video of Kat's life, you would see her involved in a variety of relationships. None of them would appear to be unhealthy or conflictual. She would seem to give relationships the kind of significance that the Bible does. But for Kat, relationships are an end, not a means to an end. For her, the people in her life are more a source of personal happiness than a tool God uses to continue the good work that he has begun in her and in them. Because of this, Kat lives in a web of relationships that seldom get below the casual. They are about weather, recipes, activities, politics, and what's happening with the children. She finds deeper relationships too intense and too much work, and she is thankful that the people in her life respect these boundaries.

Once again, the problem is not that Kat is dissatisfied with her relationships. In fact, she is way too easily satisfied. Kat has woven a fabric of little kingdom relationships around her. These relationships have little or nothing to do with God, his will for Kat, and his plan on earth. They are part of a quest for an unencumbered, low-demand, entertaining, happy life. Kat seems utterly blind to the transcendent glories that could be hers as she experiences the travails of pursuing relationships that are driven more by the purposes of God's kingdom than by little kingdom desires. Kat's short-sighted satisfaction is exposed by the fact that when she looks at her relationships, she does not groan. If you pursue God's plan for your relationships, you will groan, because you will be confronted with how far you and others are from what God says is good and best. Pursuit of big kingdom relationships will bring you to the end of yourself and make you cry out for the help that only God can provide. Like Kat, you are too easily satisfied by fun and casual relationships.

ULTIMATE FULFILLMENT

Where does one find ultimate fulfillment, satisfaction, and contentment? In God and God alone. Living for God is indeed fulfilling, but we don't find him fulfilling because we are too busy being satisfied with the temporary pleasures of the physical world. Before we ever come to God we have already decided the things that we want in order to be fulfilled. We tend to seek God so that he will deliver some kind of physical, relational, or circumstantial fulfillment. Rather than working to satisfy us with these, God wants us to experience hunger so deep that it drives us to forsake these things and finally find our satisfaction in him.

You see, God *did* create all these things. They are *not* evil in and of themselves. They exist primarily for God's glory and secondarily for our enjoyment, but they must never become the satisfaction of our hearts. Kat didn't groan. For the moment, she had found her satisfaction in the physical, relational, and circumstantial things around her, and so had shrunk the size of her life to the size of her life.

Little kingdom living is all about the satisfactions and dissatisfactions of the created world. It is about constantly pursuing what I think I need or what I think will fulfill me. These pleasures, unlike the pleasure of knowing and serving God and his purposes, tend to result in a harvest of bad fruit. Because the things of the physical earth will never truly satisfy me, they tend to leave me fat, unhealthy, and addicted; bitter, hurt, and disappointed; and angry, demanding, and controlling. Being ruled by the desire for little kingdom pleasures harms both body and soul.

So we need to redefine what it means to be ungodly. Ungodliness runs much, much deeper than a failure to keep a list of rules. Ungodliness is about my life being so dominated by desire for present pleasures that my heart will never stay inside of God's boundaries. Searching for satisfaction in what I can see, touch, taste, hear, or hold in my hands will always lead me to commit an endless list of sins of heart and behavior.

Big kingdom living is lived in the tension between deep gratitude and daily groaning. I am thankful because I have been rescued and am being progressively freed from my bondage to the unfilled promises of physical earth. I am thankful because I am learning to keep creation in its proper place. Yes, I am thankful for gorgeous flowers, sweet aromas, and the delicate taste of well-prepared food. I am thankful for the many people in my life, for sunsets and rivers, for mountains and animals. And I am thankful for how each of these things in some way reflects the glory of God. But most of all I am thankful that God has broken the power of these things over me and is teaching me not to look to them for the satisfaction of my soul.

At the same time I groan. I groan because this world is a broken place. There is nowhere I look where this brokenness cannot be seen. I groan because I am not yet all that God's grace can enable me to be. I groan because I long for God's kingdom to come. I groan because I have tasted the pleasures of this earth and they do not satisfy. Because of these things there is never a day when it is not right for me to groan.

Paul was right; groaning is the default language of the children of God. And it is this groaning that expands everything your life touches to the size of the kingdom of God.

THE FINAL QUESTION: BE HONEST. WHAT ARE THE THINGS THAT MAKE YOU GROAN?

ARE YOU MAKING MUSIC
WITH THE KING?

CHAPTER TWELVE

JAZZ

har·mo·ni·ous: suitable and fitting;
existing together in correspondence with others

THE BOTTOM LINE: GOD CALLS US TO THE VERTICALLY INTERACTIVE LIFESTYLE OF LIVING IN MOMENT-BY-MOMENT HARMONY WITH HIM.

I will never forget that night. I had gone with my brother Tedd to the University of Toledo's field hall to hear my first jazz concert. It was the Ramsey Lewis Trio. They were the hot jazz group of the moment. I simply was not prepared for what I was going to experience that night. Musically, that night changed my life!

The night started out with Ramsey Lewis on the piano, playing a song that was familiar to everyone in the audience. I must admit I was a bit disappointed. I had never heard the Ramsey Lewis Trio before, and Tedd had given them quite a buildup. We had paid a lot of money for the tickets.

As Ramsey Lewis was making his way through the first pass of this familiar tune, I kept thinking, *This is it? This is what all that big buildup was about? I could have heard this on almost any local radio station!* Then all of the sudden, as the trio launched into its second pass through the piece, something amazing happened. The three members of the group all seemed to move in a different direction. Although they were still playing the song, it didn't sound like the song anymore. But it wasn't dissonant, chaotic, or discordant; it worked! Somehow, even though they were each doing their own individual thing, they were playing together. It sounded amazing, fresh, and creative, but also harmonious.

You see, they hadn't rebelled against or abandoned the song. They were committed to that unified theme, and that made the music work. There was something each of them was zealous to do, and that kept what they were playing from degenerating into individualistic musical chaos. Even though it looked like it, they were not doing their own thing. They were committed to playing jazz. And it was this commitment, which each of them applied to their instrument in a different way, that kept the music intricate and unpredictable, but beautiful at the same time. Jazz isn't about completely trashing the rules and making up your own along the way. What makes great jazz work is that it is gloriously unpredictable and creative, while at the same time submitting itself to a set of rules.

There was a defined musical structure, a set of rules you might say, which each of the members of the trio was committed to play within. Though they were not following all of the markings on a sheet of music, they all stayed within the structure of the song (key signature, time signature, etc.), making their combined efforts unified and exhilarating. Yes, they were free to be creative, to wander, to make their own individual application of the structure to their particular instrument—as long as they stayed within the musical parameters of the song.

The night was a mind-expanding experience of the intersection of form and freedom. It was the most freeing, soaring, in-the-moment music I had ever experienced, because it submitted to a form that made it work. What I didn't get that night and sadly discovered decades later, was that what I experienced in the field hall of the University of Toledo had everything to do with the kingdom of God.

THE MUSICAL KINGDOM

God is the ultimate musician. His music transforms your life. The notes of redemption rearrange your heart and restore your life. His songs of forgiveness, grace, reconciliation, truth, hope, sovereignty, and love give you back your humanity and restore your identity. But he has ordained not to play his music alone. He calls each of us to be players in his great redemptive band. He calls each of us to play and sing the notes of hope, faith, forgiveness, and love as well. He calls for each of us to put down our music and to take up his. He calls each of us to quit composing and to start submitting. He calls us to play his music in harmony with him, and when we do this the kingdom has come into our lives.

He isn't committed to endorsing our compositions. He isn't looking for ways to help us to be happy with our own music. He isn't excited by the novel things that we may find musically fulfilling. He knows that there is one fatal flaw in the music that each of us plays. It is written by us! Our music falls apart and never reaches the heights that it was designed to reach, and for one reason. It is played outside of his structure. And so our music harms and does not heal, it divides and does not reconcile, it condemns and does not forgive, and it makes war even against the composer, the Prince of Peace.

But God doesn't rip the instrument out of our hands and throw us in a place where the music has died. By his grace, he forgives our delusionally grandiose individualism and actually invites us to make music with him. And his grace gives us the ability to play as we have never played before.

The music we now play is more beautiful than any we have ever made. It is so beautiful that it is as if he, with all his creativity and skill, is playing through us.

But with all our delight at being part of the band of redemption, we still fall into daydreaming of being the composer. Even in the face of the glory of the music of redemption, where we have played with others in ways that we wouldn't have thought possible, we still run off with our God-given instruments and play the discordant notes of autonomy and selfish desire. We still give way to playing the notes that we have written, just the way we want to play them. There are times when our ears really do get tricked, and we think that our music is more beautiful than his. There our times when we tire of the songs of redemption and crave to hear our own notes. There are times when it seems so fulfilling just to pick up our instrument and blare whatever we want to blare.

So we regularly need the Great Composer to silence our playing for a moment so that our ears can hear with wisdom how the notes we have been playing lack beauty and harmony. And he forgives us once again, inviting us to play the sweet notes of redemption, making harmonious music with him.

THE JAZZ KINGDOM

Earlier I commented that what I experienced listening to the Ramsey Lewis Trio had everything to do with the kingdom of God. Expanding your life to the size of God's kingdom has everything to do with the same *form* and *freedom* principles that the trio so deftly applied that evening. It is at the intersection of these principles that we tend to misunderstand what kingdom living actually looks like.

You do not have to obsess over what *form* your life will take if you expand everything in your life to the size of God's kingdom, because God has provided the form and structure for you. The form is his Word.

Scripture provides the parameters in which we live out the kingdom of God during our days here on earth. God knows that if we are going to make harmonious music with him we need to know who he is, who we are, what life is about. We need to know how we are to do all that we have been ordained to do, and what the goal of it all is. The narratives, principles, propositions, commands, and promises of Scripture are given by God to provide the structure in which you and I are called to live. We will only ever be what we were created to be, experience what we were created to experience, and enjoy what we were designed to enjoy when we submit to the structure of his revelation. The song of Scripture provides the musical structure for all the little kingdom songs that he equips us to play in our friendships, families, churches, and communities. And when we do this, the kingdom of God, in all of its glorious harmony, comes to that place.

Though we are made in his image and so are creatures with amazing gifts, we were not made to write our own musical form. No, we are called to exercise our dexterity within the form that he has so lovingly provided for us in his Word. And, like the trio that evening, being committed to playing within the structure of God's revelation doesn't crush our creativity. Rather, it becomes the context in which our creativity can soar to heights previously unimagined.

Our kingdom calling is to live out of a dedicated, disciplined, and persevering daily commitment to only make music that is in harmony with the Composer, because it lives within the structure of his revelation. When we do this, our thoughts, desires, words, and actions, like his, have the power to help, restore, reconcile, and give hope. When we play music with him, what we do and say actually has the power to transform individual lives and whole communities. You see, it is only the music of redemption that can ever do the work of restoration that this broken world so desperately needs. It is only the strains of grace that are able to make all things new.

When we are playing his music, our notes are the notes of justice, mercy, peace, love, and hope. These notes embrace the poor and the rich, the young and the old, men and women, and boys and girls. They are not restricted to a certain geographic, economic, ethnic, language, or historical setting. The notes of redemption are universal in their application and global in their power. And when we play them, our lives transcend the narrow confines of our claustrophobic hopes and dreams. When we make harmonious music with him, we become part of the eternal song. This song was written before the foundation of the earth was laid, and it will still be played a trillion years after time is no more! When we make music within the form that he has laid down, our lives transcend the boundaries of our lives and become part of something that is huge and significant. When we do this, we live for a greater glory than the sound of our own notes, and in so doing get back our humanity.

THE NOISE OF DISHARMONY

Joey had gotten to the place where he hated to go home after work. The acrimony between him and Emma was so intense it took his breath away. Driving up their street toward home, he could feel the nervous tension build as his grip tightened on the steering wheel. He just knew that there would be something—something he said or something he forgot to do— and it would be the match to light another explosion.

It hadn't always been this way. There had been a time when he and Emma loved to be together, when they hung on one another's words. But the surface harmony of those first few months of marriage was short lived. Joey and Emma didn't know it, but they were writing and playing their own individual pieces of music. Each had had a dream of what their marriage would be like. Each had expectations for the other. And each was disappointed and angry at how far their marriage was from what they had dreamed it would be.

The difficulty started with little moments of disharmony. But those little moments of disharmony had grown so discordant that their relationship was more like the chaotic noise of traffic than a well-written and well-played duet. Here were two people living together who wanted their own way and who refused to give way. The tension they experienced, they had created. The disharmony they hated, they made. They could be playing the kind of music that is only fully experienced when the notes you play are in harmony with the Great Composer. Joey and Emma do not have to live this way. There is grace for just this kind of disharmonious relationship. There is hope for Joey and Emma, but to experience it, they must be willing to give up their own music.

When we attempt to write and play our own music, bad things happen. Our self-focus, self-pleasing notes result in division and disharmony. They damage souls and crush hearts. They destroy hope. They lead to violence and despair. They break up families and leave communities in crumbled ruins. They pervert justice and leave government corrupt. They weaken the body of Christ and make all of us lame. When everyone in a family, friendship, or community is writing his own music or playing her own notes, that place will be a place of brokenness, division, intolerance, anger recrimination, discouragement, fear. When we do this, all of the healing communities that God has designed (family, church, government) become so diseased that they are able to provide healing for no one. When we write our own music, the kingdom of self comes to that place, interfering with the sweet music of shalom that the Great Composer so wonderfully wrote.

BUT IT'S JAZZ!

The harmonious music of the kingdom that God calls us to play with him is not just about form; it is about *freedom* as well. Think about it: the revelation of God in his Word is not like sheet music. That is, God doesn't give you every note on the page that you are to play, as if all you have to do is to play them. The Bible simply doesn't address every specific situation or relationship in which you may find yourself. God hasn't pre-scripted every conversation for you or pre-made all of your decisions. If that's true, you may be asking, what *has* God given us in his Word? What we have been given in the pages of Scripture is a key signature and a time signature. As long as we stay within those divinely composed parameters, we are free to improvise with him.

You can't reduce the great historical moments, the great narrative themes, the instructional wisdom, and the great principles and commands of the Bible to sheet music. They just don't function that way.

Consider, for example, that you can list out all the direct commands that God makes to moms and dads about parenting their children on two sides of a sheet of notebook paper. You aren't given a script for the conversation with your toddler who is refusing to eat, or a script for solving that sibling rivalry, or a script for helping a self-absorbed teenager see his heart. What you are given are very important parameters for each of those conversations, and you are invited by the Great Composer to make redemptive jazz inside of that structure. When you stay within the structure, your creativity is redemptive, resulting in long-term personal benefit.

There is something more to be said about our freedom to improvise inside of the composer's form. The jazz lifestyle of the kingdom of God is a *communal freedom.* Jazz musicians make harmonious music, not just because they stay inside an agreed upon musical structure, but because they play in community with one another. Good jazz musicians are not just good players; they are also very skilled listeners. Their jazz is always an interaction with what is going on around them. God hasn't given us sheet music. He has composed a structure that liberates us to improvise within the structure, and all while listening intently to one another and to him. What is he doing in and through my brothers and sisters in this moment? How can I make music that is harmonious with what God is intending, and with what others need? These are the questions of the communal freedom of the kingdom of God.

JAZZ WITH A PURPOSE

Now you may be asking, "Why would God, the source of ultimate wisdom, not give us the complete sheet music for everyone's life in every situation and relationship they will ever encounter? He knows what is going to happen in every second of our existence. Wouldn't this have been phenomenally easier?" Consider the question for a moment. Why does this idea of utter predictability tend to be so attractive to us? Is it not because what our sinful hearts really long for is comfort, ease, success, and control? These desires are not wrong in and of themselves, but their danger is that they tend to compete with the one thing we were created to pursue and enjoy. The dangerous dependency of creative and harmonious music-making with God is the only place we will ever become truly and fully human.

You see, God has designed his Word and his kingdom in such a way that they both drive us to him in moment-by-moment dependency. What he wants for us and from us is much more than dogged obedience to a set of standards. What he wants is us! He wants to be the treasure of our hearts and the joy of our souls. He wants to know the same community with us that he has known with himself in the Trinity. He is after relationship with us! So, he gives us just what we need. We know the key that we are to play, and he has revealed to us what the time signature is, but he has not told us exactly what to do and say in all the moments of life where we will be making music with him. And he does this because he wants us to seek him, pray to him, and rely on him as we are improvising our way through life.

He wants us to be spontaneous and creative. He wants each new moment to be a fresh experience of faith and grace. He wants us to exercise the full range of the gifts that he has given us. He wants us to transcend the boundaries of our shrink-wrapped little worlds. He wants us to be connected to what is holy, infinite, and eternal. He wants us to be as fully human as his image-bearers were meant to be. But he wants all of these things to be the harmonious result of intimate, responsive, dependent, and joyful community with him. That's why he hasn't given us sheet music and sent us off on our own. He has called us to the unsettling freedom of a lifestyle of redemptive improvisational jazz. And this jazz lifestyle only works when we are paying careful attention to what he has composed and to what he is playing at the moment.

Every time you make creative, interactive, and harmonious jazz with your Redeemer, whether in your home, friendships, community, church, or at work, while staying inside of his parameters, you are expanding what you touch to the size of God's kingdom.

THE FINAL QUESTION: WHERE IN YOUR LIFE ARE
YOU TEMPTED TO WRITE YOUR OWN MUSIC RATHER
THAN MAKING HARMONIOUS MUSIC WITH THE KING?

ARE YOU WILLING TO ASK
FOR FORGIVENESS?

CHAPTER THIRTEEN

FORGIVENESS

*con·fes·sion: an acknowledgment of guilt
by one who is charged with an offense*

THE BOTTOM LINE: BIG KINGDOM LIVING IS ALL ABOUT THE HUMILITY OF SEEKING FORGIVENESS AND THE GRACE OF GRANTING IT.

Sam knew he was wrong. He knew that what he had said and done was not only inappropriate; it was sin. Several times Sam had left work early and had someone punch his time card for him. He rationalized that people who knew about the recent birth of his twins would understand. And he knew that he was not the only one doing it. But he alone had been caught. No matter how many rationalizations he test-marketed in his own mind, he could not defend his actions.

It was just a matter of time before he would have to eat crow and admit his errors, but it was so hard. He wanted to turn the table and point his finger at all the other sinners in the room. He wanted to remind people of all the tough things that were on his plate. He wished he could have the opportunity to convince people of what a good guy he generally was. But it all seemed like feeding a single peanut to a very hungry elephant. None of it satisfied the emptiness inside. He had to go and confess his wrong and ask for forgiveness. As he walked to his boss's office, he still searched for an excuse and wanted to rat on everyone, but he knew he couldn't.

Why is it so hard for us to admit that we are wrong? Why is it so hard to ask for forgiveness? Because we all like to think we are more righteous than we actually are. And all of us are better at seeing the sin of others than we are our own. But there is more going on here. I am deeply persuaded that our struggle with forgiveness is a kingdom struggle.

MY WILL, MY WAY

Did you ever wonder why protests are so attractive to a human being? When I participate in a protest over some issue, I am able to say that this particular problem somehow exists outside of me. And since I am not the problem here, I get to point the finger at you, publicly exposing your wrongs that are affecting me and others. What makes protesting so exhilarating and intoxicating is being righteous. For once I get to say, "I am innocent here, and I am frankly outraged at the wrong that you are doing!" If you invited people to two events, one to protest something and the other to confess something, which gathering do you think would draw the bigger crowd?

Asking for forgiveness is so hard because of what it says about life and what it says about me. You cannot ask for forgiveness without acknowledging that there is something in life that is more important than the progress of your own kingdom. You cannot seek forgiveness without owning the fact that you were created for the glory of another. You cannot make honest, humble confession without acknowledging that there are more important things in life than getting your own way and being happy. You cannot admit a wrong without being hit with the fact that there are bigger things in life than how you feel and how you feel about how you feel. You see, it's our sturdy allegiance to our own kingdom that makes us unwilling to confess that we have gotten in the way of God's kingdom on earth.

Why would you ever yell at someone? Why would you ever hold a grudge? Why would you ever struggle to serve another person? Why would you ever find it hard to be patient and forbearing? Why would you find it hard to celebrate the success of another? Why would you ever speak a word of gossip? Why would you ever be tempted to steal what is not yours? Why would you ever misuse sex or food? Why would you envy the power, position, or possessions of another?

Why, parent, do you struggle with anger at the very child whose birth was such a miracle of fulfillment? Why, wife, can the person whose presence once made you tingle, irritate you so just by the way he chews his food? Why, husband, would you ever get annoyed in the middle of a conversation with someone you were once delighted to commit to spending your life with?

Why would you ever wallow in self-pity? Why would you ever let bitterness hold you in its grip? What would make you feel like quitting or cause you to dread the next day? Why would you ever grow cynical and walk away from another human being? We do these things because we want our own way.

My allegiance to my own kingdom is deep in the DNA of my sinful nature, causing me to be self-centered, self-righteous, condemning, and impatient. I know what I want. I know what will make me happy. I have a vision for what my life could be like, and you are constantly getting in the way of the plans and purposes of my kingdom. Now, I am not just talking about the big situations and decisions of life. You don't live in those moments very often. No, this personal kingdom, personal happiness, don't-get-in-the-way-of-what-I-want spiritual dynamic, which is the struggle of every sinner, lives with subtle drama in the little moments of daily life. That is why you are mad when you can't get in the bathroom when you want to, or when someone takes your parking space, or when you don't get the recognition that you think you deserve.

Asking for forgiveness is hard because you have to admit to why you need it so frequently. It is hard because you have to face the fact that with all of your growth in grace, biblical literacy, ministry experience, and theological acumen, you still revert again and again to the pursuit of your own kingdom interests. When you seek forgiveness, you are confessing that you still forget why you were put on earth and granted the amazing gift of God's grace. You are admitting that you forget that every gift you have been given is to be invested in his kingdom.

THE FORGIVENESS KINGDOM

Seeking forgiveness is always the result of having another kingdom in view. You are owning the fact that you were not made for you. When you live for you, you forget God and his kingdom and travel outside the boundaries of his will. Not only that, but every time you ask for forgiveness from God or people, you are admitting that you are part of the massive problem that the big kingdom addresses. The golden offer of the kingdom of God is forgiveness. This is why Jesus told his disciples to preach a message of repentance as they announced the kingdom. God establishes his kingdom so that all that sin has broken can be fully and completely restored. In the center of the kingdom of God, you do not find a gargantuan palace inhabited by an unapproachable king. No, in the center of the kingdom of God is a bloody cross, on which hung a broken King, who welcomes us as we are. This King did not demand righteousness from us, for if he did, none of us would ever be qualified to live in his kingdom. No, he was righteous for us, and although he was a king, he willingly took our criminal's death so that we might be forgiven. What this

King demands is confession, and in the moment when we confess, we are liberated from our bondage to ourselves and freed to live for another.

Those who have been welcomed into the big kingdom have been welcomed into a lifestyle of forgiveness. It is a way of living where each day I admit that I instinctively get in the way of what God is doing on earth. I do it as an individual. I do it in my marriage and parenting. I do it in my friendships. I do it at work. I do it in the body of Christ. I do it in my neighborhood. When I live this lifestyle I find joy in telling Jesus, day after day, that I need what he did in his life, death, and resurrection. This lifestyle is about growing to acknowledge that in some way, every day, I give evidence to the fact that the cross was necessary. And this lifestyle of forgiveness makes my daily attitude one of heartfelt gratitude and joy. Even though I have challenged his kingship and thought that I would make a better king, he has not rejected me or condemned me. No, he has wrapped his forgiving arms around me and invited me to be part of something infinitely more beautiful than anything I would have ever chosen for myself.

GETTING IT RIGHT

When you ask for forgiveness, you really do get it right. The fact that you can have an accurate view of yourself is a living demonstration of how powerful the grace of Christ really is. The grace of Christ has the power to open your blind eyes to see. It has the power to pry open your clinched-fisted hold on your own will and cling to the cause of a better kingdom. And it has the power to help you gladly confess what you once refused even to see! When you ask for forgiveness you really do get it right, because you are letting go of your will and celebrating his, you are giving up on your righteousness and rejoicing in his, and you are running from your kingdom into his.

FORGIVENESS IS WAR

It's hard to ask for forgiveness because asking for forgiveness is war. It's a war between self-righteousness and unearned grace. It's a war between the rules of my kingdom and the commandments of the King. It's a war between a desire to be served and the call to freely love and willingly serve. It's a war between living for my own little moments of glory and being consumed by the glory of God. This war is fought every day on the turf of my heart. But I do not fight this war alone. The King, who has welcomed me into his better kingdom, is a Warrior King who will continue to fight on my behalf until the last enemy is under his feet.

This means there is hope for me even though I lose sight of the big kingdom and regress back into the kingdom of self. There is hope for me even though I would rather fight for fifteen seconds of self-glory than to give him the glory that actually belongs to him. There is hope for me even though I would rather win an argument than reconcile a relationship. There is hope for me even though I would rather fantasize about vengeance than grant quick forgiveness. There is hope for me even though I am good at focusing on your sin while forgetting my own. There is hope for me because I do not fight for my soul alone. The King fights for me, and every time I ask for forgiveness he has won another battle on my behalf.

You see, this *is* the battle of battles. This *is* the conflict that lurks below every other conflict we experience. This *is* the thing in all of us that God refuses to accommodate. His kingdom *will* come. His will *will* be done. He will not sit idly by and permit his kingdom children to live with a greater practical allegiance to the building of their own kingdoms. So he fights for the freedom of our souls. He battles for the control of our hearts. He works to liberate our desires and to focus our thoughts. And as he does this, he calls us to humbly confess that we really do love ourselves more than we love him and others. He invites us to admit how regularly we demand our own way. He welcomes us to own up to our anger, greed, envy, and vengeance. If his kingdom is ever to fully and completely come, it must be a kingdom of forgiveness where rebel citizens can be made right again and again and again.

FORGIVENESS AND THE BIG KINGDOM

Every time you ask for forgiveness, you get it right.

Every time you ask for forgiveness, you step out of your little kingdom and into his.

Every time you ask for forgiveness, you say that the Bible's description of you and everyone around you is accurate.

Every time you ask for forgiveness, you declare that your life does not belong to you, but has been created for the purpose of Another.

Every time you ask for forgiveness, you say that selfishness is your biggest sin and that grace is your only hope.

Every time you ask for forgiveness, you are reminding yourself who you are and what you truly need.

Every time you ask for forgiveness, you refuse to be comfortable with your rebellion.

Every time you ask for forgiveness, you recognize that the biggest problems you face in life exist inside of you, not outside of you.

Every time you ask for forgiveness, you are praying that God's kingdom would come and his will would be done on earth as it is in heaven.

Every time you ask for forgiveness, you make the kingdom of God visible for others to see.

Every time you ask for forgiveness, you are worshipping the King of forgiveness and encouraging others to do the same.

Every time you ask for forgiveness, your sight is accurate, your head is clear, and your heart is in the right place.

Every time you ask for forgiveness, you cry out for an eternity when forgiveness has finished its work once and for all.

Every time you ask for forgiveness, you tell yourself that for all the good you have experienced in God's kingdom, there is still more that is needed and more to come.

A lifestyle of seeking forgiveness expands everything you are touching to the size of God's kingdom.

THE FINAL QUESTION: DO YOU FIND JOY IN THE LIBERATING LIFESTYLE OF SEEKING FORGIVENESS?

ARE YOU AN
INSATIABLE ROMANTIC?

CHAPTER FOURTEEN

LONELINESS

ro·mance: an ardent emotional involvement,
a fascination or enthusiasm for someone

THE BOTTOM LINE: LIFE IN THE KINGDOM OF GOD IS LIKE WAITING FOR THE LOVE OF YOUR LIFE TO RETURN.

It was going to be a month-long trip to Korea and India. I was excited about the many ministry opportunities and challenges that were before me. I felt privileged to be doing what I was doing. At the airport I said a long, sweet goodbye to my lover and my lifelong best friend, Luella. She was a bit tearful; it was a long trip, and she knew that I would be far away and often unreachable. I was ready to embark on a journey that it seemed I had been preparing for for years. As I walked down the concourse, I kept looking back for one last glance at her. I remember being halfway down the walkway and looking one more time and being disappointed because the crowd had obscured Luella. She was gone.

The flight was long, and I couldn't wait for my feet to touch earth and my body to find a soft bed. As I was digging through my suitcase that first night, I discovered a piece of chocolate that Luella had hidden away with a typical Luella note. I went to sleep with a smile on my face at what she had sent with me to make my journey easier. Although Luella was physically in Philadelphia, I had taken her with me and she had left pieces of herself behind for me to remember and enjoy.

As the days of separation increased, I found myself thinking about Luella more and more. In fact, there were moments when not only would I wish she were there to share the experience with me, but I would start to turn and say something to her, only to be jolted into the reality that I had left her at home. By the time I passed the midway point of my trip, I was counting down the days. I found myself daydreaming about getting off the plane and seeing her face. I envisioned the first sight of her, the first touch of her hand, the first kiss. I thought about sitting across a table from her and going through a detailed chronology of the trip. With my heart I saw her smile and I heard her laugh.

I began talking more about Luella to those who were with me. I wasn't conscious of it, but I found ways to squeeze her into the conversation and sing her praises. Finally someone said to me, "You really miss her, don't you?"

On those final days of the trip it was hard to concentrate. I politely did my duty, but my heart was not in it. I wanted to get on the plane and make my way home. And the closer the day came, the lonelier I got. I just wanted to be home with Luella.

A CENTRAL ROMANCE

What drives our life in the kingdom of God? What motivates its activity and fuels its duty? What is the one indispensable ingredient that immediately separates it from life in the little kingdom of self? I can answer these questions with one word: *romance.* Now, maybe you're thinking, *Paul, what in the world are you talking about? What does expanding my life to the size of the kingdom of God have to do with romance? I could understand if you had said theology or ministry, but romance? I just don't get it.*

As I watch the church operate, as I look back on my own life with the Lord, and as I look at the Bible and how it describes the Christian lifestyle, I am more and more persuaded that there is one central thing, one foundational pursuit, one unchallenged heart that must lie behind it all. And if it doesn't, nothing will be as it was meant to be in the big kingdom. That thing is not an unwavering commitment to a consistently biblical theology. It is not working to build a comprehensive Christian world- and life-view through which you look at everything in life. It is not a dedicated pursuit of involvement in the fellowship of the body of Christ. It is not a life shaped by a persevering commitment to ministry and service. And it is not a zeal for daily personal devotion, study, and worship. This one central thing is not so much a pursuit, a habit, or a duty, but a passionate disposition of the heart.

Behind every good thing that the King calls us to do, the one thing that will give us motivation and direction is this central and abiding romance. It is meant to be the one holy romance of our lives, the romance for which we were both created and redeemed: Christ's great cosmic love for us and our responsive love for him. At the center of the kingdom is the King; and therefore the center of kingdom living is a deep, abiding, life-shaping affection for the King. This one central love fuels everything else we are meant to pursue as we exit the narrow confines of our self-defined kingdoms and begin to enjoy life in the big sky country of the kingdom of God. We are simply meant to be madly in love with Christ. He is meant to be the thing that occupies our minds and fills our hearts. He is meant to be what excites us and brings us joy. He is to be the One whom we are living to please. You really will expand your life to the size of the kingdom of God when you heart is absolutely captured by this one central romance.

At its core, life in the big kingdom is not so much about pursuing a thing; it is about pursuing a person. It is about having the eyes of my heart focused on Christ. It is about a soul that is filled with appreciation and brimming with affection. It is walking around astounded that he would place his affection on me and even receive my flawed love. It is living with the hope that someday we will no longer be separated; someday I will be united to him and live with him forever.

In the meantime, life in the big kingdom is not just about being thankful for his provision, for fellowship, sound teaching, and worthwhile causes to give my energies to. No, central to big kingdom living is being thankful for *him*; for *his* presence, *his* forgiveness, *his* patience, *his* mercy, *his* gentleness, *his* wisdom, *his* compassion, *his* companionship, *his* kindness, and *his* love. Big kingdom living is about feeling incredibly blessed, not just because of the physical things, the beneficial circumstances, and the many people who have been placed in my life, but feeling blessed because of him. I cannot believe that he would love me! I cannot believe that the King of kings, the Creator, the Savior, and the Ruler of the universe would ever desire to be my friend. And I live with grateful amazement at the lengths to which he went to have this love relationship with me. It is this one central romance that gives motivation and direction to every other good thing that defines what it means to live for God's kingdom and glory. And when your heart is not captured by this love, no matter how many external Christian pursuits you are giving yourself to, you are still actually living in the little kingdom.

NO TIME FOR ROMANCE

We are so distractible. We are so fickle. We are so incredibly busy. We live at such a frenetic pace. There are so many ways we have found to fill our days, yes even our lives. Could it be that we keep ourselves so busy, so on the run, so distracted by the events of the day, or by the plans of the days to come, that we have little or no time to pursue this one central romance?

Could it be that we have been welcomed to a love relationship with Christ, which by ourselves we would have never pursued or could have never deserved, but now are too overcommitted to run after and enjoy?

Relationships take commitment. Relationships demand time. Relationships require perseverance. Relationships call us to sacrifice. At its core, biblical faith is not a commitment to an ideology; it is an undeserved welcome into a relationship. It is Christ making us the "apple of his eye" and calling us to love him more than anything or anyone else in our lives. Can you imagine a man declaring his love for a woman, telling her that she is more important than anything else in his life, and yet finding little time to deepen their communion and love? It is possible for us to declare ourselves to be Christians, to say that we love the Lord more than we love anything else, and yet to have no time for Christ!

It is frighteningly easy to find so much satisfaction in the things we are doing that we have little time or energy to find satisfaction in Jesus. The problem is that few of the things we are pursuing are harmful in themselves. We can give ourselves valid reasons for being involved in all of them. And so the distractions in our lives don't trouble us. They occupy our schedules with logic and plausibility, even though they prevent us from pursuing this one central romance that is meant to be the unchallenged source of our meaning, identity, purpose, and hope.

Our schedules are filled by:

exercising,

night classes,

music lessons,

theater,

shopping,

vacations,

second jobs,

home decorating,

golf,

Little League,

concerts,

restaurants,

remodeling,

politics,

television,

hair appointments,

iPods,

museums,

doctor appointments,

budget balancing,

VCRs,

amusement parks,

walking the dog,

conferences,

reading,

cooking classes,

and on and on....

Is it possible that we can sing of our love for Christ on Sunday, but have no time for this one central romance on Monday? Could it be that we have filled our time with too many things? Could it be that we are not frustrated captives of our busy schedules, but are, in fact, the heart-driven controllers of our time? Might our schedules actually portray what is important to us and gives us joy?

At the epicenter of the kingdom of God is a love relationship with Christ, a deep affection for Jesus that guides and shapes everything you are, everything you think, everything you desire, every decision you make, every word you say, and every action you take. Jesus *is* the kingdom! His kingdom is first a kingdom of love! His welcome to the kingdom is actually an invitation to an eternal love relationship with him.

Now, does this sound mystical and impractical to you? Does it seem too ethereal to really connect to your everyday life? Well, let me remind you that for all the powerful emotions and magic moments of a human romance, a healthy love relationship is actually pretty mundane and practical. You have to make the practical commitments of time, money, affection, and energy. You have to listen well and speak clearly. You have to be determined to be patient, forgiving, forbearing, and humble. You need to recognize the places giving and serving are needed. You have to take time to call, write, email, or text. And you have to decide what things you will give up in order to do all of these things. The health of this relationship will not depend on three or four big significant moments, but on ten thousand little moments where you did the loving thing. So it is with our relationship with Christ. It is the grand affection that is lived out in thousands of little choices and actions. When we are serious about our love of Christ, our lives will show it.

FICKLE HEARTS

When we examine our lives closely, it becomes clear that our problem is not our schedules. It is not that God has put more on our plates than we can possibly accomplish in seven, twenty-four-hour days. Our problem is our fickle hearts that wander away from this one central romance and so easily give our affection to another. The Bible calls this *love of the world.* And the Bible tells us that if we love the world, the love of the father is not in us. (See 1 John 2:15–17.) James says that we get angry with one another because we are spiritual adulterers, and the person next to us gets in the way of what we love. (See James 4:1–4.) The world is so attractive to our eyes and so seductive to our hearts. The creation can seem so much more real than the Creator. The sights, sounds, touches, and tastes of the world can seem to make us more alive than the purposes, promises, presence, and provisions of a God who can neither be seen nor heard. This is a battle you do not win once. It is a battle that you must face every day. You must tell yourself that in this world you are surrounded by other lovers who will seek to woo you away from the one grand romance that is to be the core of your existence. You must prepare for this seduction and you must steel yourself against the temptation to spiritual adultery. And you must do it again and again and again, or your heart will be stolen away.

LONELINESS

If love for Jesus really is the central affection of your life, if he owns your heart and commands your thoughts, and if knowing and pleasing him is the one determined pursuit of your life, then you will live a lonely life. Yes, you will be thankful for all the wonderful fellow romancers that God has put in your life. You will be thankful for every moment of human understanding, patience, gentleness, and compassion that you are blessed to experience. You will find joy in your relationships in the body of Christ. But your heart will long for the day when you will actually be in his presence forever. Living in the big kingdom is like waiting for the one you love to come home. When separated from your earthly lover, your loneliness surfaces in various ways:

- It's sometimes hard to concentrate because you're thinking of him.
- You look for ways to squeeze him into a conversation.
- You brag about his characteristics and accomplishments wherever you can.
- You find yourself swinging between nostalgia and anxious expectation.
- You rehearse what you will say when you first see him again, altering the lines until they best describe your love, excitement, and joy.
- You regretfully relive all of your thoughtless, selfish, and hurtful moments, wishing you could pluck each one of them out of history.
- You resolve to love him better with every passing day.

- You are comforted by the assurance that even though he is away, he has promised unshakable love and a guaranteed return.
- You read and reread everything he has written you, analyzing every word for every drop of meaning and memorizing every passage that gives you hope.
- You seek the company of his friends because in them you find vestiges of him.
- You take personally any attack against him, and you try to clarify any misunderstandings anyone may have about his character or actions.

Why do you do all of these things? Because you are lonely for the one you love, and you refuse to numb the ache in your heart by letting anyone or anything else take his place while you wait for his return. Christian life is meant to be marked by an ache of deep spiritual loneliness. The Christian life is meant to be shaped by an eye that is constantly on eternity and the amazing reunion that is to come. That's why Scripture repeatedly describes the Christian life as a life of waiting. (See Rom. 8:23–25; Gal. 5:5; 1 Thess. 1:9–10; Heb. 9:28.) Our problem is not that we fail to be satisfied. Our problem is that we are too quickly satisfied. When we are not lonely, it is because present lovers have stolen our affection away, and for the moment, we are satisfied.

Big kingdom living is supposed to look like waiting for the love of your life to return. You are waiting, but in your wait you are actively doing everything you can to deepen your love and prepare yourself for the reunion that is to come. And as you do all of that, there is an ache in your heart, because you really do want to be with the one you love forever.

THE FINAL QUESTION: WHERE IN YOUR LIFE ARE THE "OTHER LOVERS" THAT COMPETE WITH YOUR LOVE FOR CHRIST?

WHAT IS YOUR
TRUE TREASURE?

CHAPTER FIFTEEN

SACRIFICE

trea·sure: a valuable or precious possession of any kind

THE BOTTOM LINE: JESUS CALLS US TO OFFER HIM EVERYTHING SO THAT WE CAN BE FREE FROM THE THINGS THAT HAVE A HOLD ON US.

Do you know that every day you and I make personal sacrifices for something? This is hard to admit, but Luella and I got hooked on watching the reality TV show, *Dancing with the Stars*. The premise of the show was that ordinary entertainment personalities with little or no dancing experience would be paired with professional dancers in a ballroom dancing competition. For the previously non-dancing celebrities, the contest basically requires them to put their life on hold. Each week they are responsible for learning, mastering, and performing a new and complicated dance. At first you see the contestant bowled over by the catalog of dances they must learn and how specific the steps of each are. It would be hard enough just to learn how to properly dance the waltz, but imagine adding the tango, quickstep, Paso Doble, foxtrot, samba, jive, rumba, and the cha-cha!

Although these dances look fluid, delicate, and lyrical when danced correctly, they are all physically demanding and exhausting. They tend to tear up your feet, leave your toes bleeding, and cause your muscles to scream at you in sinewy protest. The dances are mentally demanding as well. You not only have to remember a series of complicated steps that tend to repeat and build, but you have to remember certain dictates of body posture as well. The way you position your head, neck, shoulders, arms, hands, hips, and toes either makes the dance look beautiful, strained, or ridiculous.

To begin with zero dance experience and then quickly become competition-ready demands an amazing level of commitment, discipline, and personal sacrifice. It means being in the dance studio from early morning until late at night. It means getting rid of all the other things on your schedule and forgetting that you have a social life. It means pushing your body beyond any limits previously set for it. It means forcing your already-confused mind to think, understand, and remember. It means starting the process all over again the next week, even though judges mocked your last hard-fought performance. And it means smiling into the camera when all you really want to do is cry, yell, or punch the nearest wall.

As we have watched this competition week after week, we have been amazed at the sacrifice. It is a whole-body, whole-mind, all-the-time competition. You cannot quit because you are tired, angry, confused, in pain, embarrassed, or bored with it all. And as soon as you complete the arduous process of learning a particular dance, you have no time to celebrate because you are required to start the process all over and learn another.

Why are these celebrities willing to make such intense personal, mental, and physical sacrifices? The answer astounded me when I thought about it. They do all of this for the dramatically short-term benefit of a little

TV exposure, bragging rights, and a modest cash prize!

We human beings are interesting characters. When we have set our hearts on something, we are willing to make incredible sacrifices to get it. Do you realize how many willing personal sacrifices you make every day? It is amazing the kind of sacrifices a person will make for a job. A person will arrive at work early, stay late, and work on the weekend, not because the boss forces them to, but in order to get that raise or promotion. It is remarkable what a person will do to get the acceptance, respect, appreciation, or love of another human being. We will hang on that person's every whim, submit our schedule to theirs, and invest time, money, and energy in pleasing them. It is incredible to watch what a person will do to turn their home into the home of their dreams. We will borrow inordinate amounts of money, spend amazing amounts of time, and have seemingly endless conversations with contractors, carpenters, and designers. We will live with dust and chaos everywhere, relegate ourselves to camping out in the tiny portion of the house that isn't being renovated, and allow the final cost to progressively escalate. For what? So that we can live in a house that is as we envisioned it could be.

I could multiply example after example. Think of the sacrifices a person will make to lose weight, have a comfortable retirement, afford that special vacation, look younger, go to that renowned restaurant just once, get a degree, have a muscular physique, be an expert cook, have good teeth, afford the special pair of shoes, own a painting, acquire an iPod and all the accessories, satisfy some kind of physical appetite, own beautiful furniture, master a subject, learn a language, own that certain car, excel in a sport, visit a long-lost relative or friend, fish or hunt, get a politician elected, attend a concert, protest social injustice, or simply get away from it all and relax. What are you sacrificing for right now?

You can't divide human beings into the "those who make sacrifices" and "those who don't." We all carry things in our hearts for which we are very willing to make sacrifices. The issue that divides us is for what, or for whom, are we willing to make these personal sacrifices.

THE SACRIFICIAL KINGDOM

For all of its joy and celebration and for all of its gifts of life and grace, the kingdom of God is a kingdom of sacrifice. The central event in the history of this kingdom is a shocking and unthinkable sacrifice. This moment of sacrifice confounded the followers who were there to see it and has interested theologians ever since. It is at once the most terrible and most beautiful event in the kingdom. It is a sacrifice that makes perfect sense and no sense at all. And this sacrifice forms the operating agenda of the kingdom from that time on.

Jesus, by his bleeding and broken body on the cross, not only gave the kingdom of God its life and hope, but its paradigm for living as well. That history-changing death on the cross is also the life-changing call of Christ to everyone who would follow him. And as it did on the cross, that willingness to die will always result in life. This kingdom is a kingdom of the cross, and everyone who celebrates that sacrifice is called to drag a cross along with them every day.

POTS OF GOLD

We've all heard of the search for the proverbial pot of gold at the end of the rainbow, but the fact is that all of us live in search of some personally prized pot of gold. Here is the principle: *behind every personal sacrifice is a quest for some kind of treasure.* This principle not only explains the life and death of Christ, but Christ's call to us as well.

> Suppose one of you wants to build a tower. Will he not first sit
> down and estimate the cost to see if he has enough money to

complete it? For if he lays the foundation and is not able to finish it, everyone who sees it will ridicule him, saying, "This fellow began to build and was not able to finish."

Or suppose a king is about to go to war against another king. Will he not first sit down and consider whether he is able with ten thousand men to oppose the one coming against him with twenty thousand? If he is not able, he will send a delegation while the other is still a long way off and will ask for terms of peace. In the same way, any of you who does not give up everything he has cannot be my disciple.

—LUKE 14:28–33

When you read this passage, you have to ask yourself why Christ asks all of his disciples to sacrifice *everything*. Think about it. He doesn't just ask for some of our things. He doesn't ask for the majority of our things. He doesn't say, "I want the best of your things." He doesn't warn us that there are going to be times when he will take precious things from us. No, his call from the outset is this: "Any of you who does not give up everything that he has cannot be my disciple." Why is his call so all-inclusive?

Jesus looks at the large crowd and does not just see people who have been attracted to his ministry because of his miracles and the authority with which he taught. He also sees people in the midst of a raging personal war. He understands that each one of the people surrounding him is a worshipper. That means that each of their lives is always shaped by the pursuit of the treasure that has come to rule their hearts. He knows that what they treasure will shape their decisions, actions, and words. And he knows that they will make incredible personal sacrifices to get, keep, and enjoy whatever it is that they treasure. So, in asking his followers to sacrifice everything, he is not calling them to live without anything. No, he is calling them to empty themselves of every other treasure but him. He is saying, "If you are going to be my disciple, I must be the treasure that gives shape and direction to everything you decide, say, and do."

Christ is asking us to search our lives for pots of gold. He wants us to look for those things that challenge the place in our hearts that only he is supposed to have. You see, Jesus demands everything, not just so we would submit to his control, but to free us from the control of things that were never designed to control us. This hard call is at the same time a call of grace. Jesus knows that we all tend to shrink our lives to the size of our lives. He knows that we all tend to exchange the spiritual for the physical. He knows that every one of us ends up in some way putting the creation in the place where only the Creator should be. And he knows that true faith, in its essence, is not about theological knowledge or ministry activity. True faith is about what your heart treasures. A true follower of Jesus holds him as the central treasure of his heart and so is willing to make significant personal sacrifices in pursuit of him.

WHITE-KNUCKLE LIVING

Where in your life right now are your fists clenched and your knuckles white? You know the scene: Someone is trying to take something from a person, and that person has wrapped his fingers so tightly around this prized possession that his knuckles are white from the force. What is it that you are holding onto tightly? Where are your knuckles white? Maybe it's your job. Perhaps it is more central to your identity, meaning, and purpose than you thought it was. Maybe it's a certain relationship to which you have attached your happiness and well-being. Maybe it's an achievement, possession, or position. Examine your living. What are the things that battle for the place that only the Lord is to have?

The thing that is shocking about Christ's call to sacrifice is that he is calling us to die. No, not to take our lives in the physical sense, but to so fundamentally sacrifice all that is precious to us, that it is as if we have died. In the sense that it cannot be the central treasure of our hearts, he calls us to die to our most precious relationship. He calls us to die to our plan for our own lives. He calls us to die to all the things we have set our hearts on that we think will make us happy and once and for all satisfy us. He calls us to open up our fists and give up all those other treasures that would control our decisions, determine our actions, and edit our words. Jesus knows we are not able to follow him and hold our fists around these things at the same time, because they end up taking hold of us.

Christ calls us to acknowledge that what we once wanted, and then became convinced that we needed, we now have become addicted to. We don't hold things very well. Again and again we experience that what we once held loosely has now come to control us. So he calls us to open our hands and offer everything for his taking. And we celebrate his call to sacrifice, because it is a welcome to freedom. This call to die is a welcome to a wonderful new life. And the One who makes this call is the One who gave himself as the sacrifice that is the central event of the big kingdom. He was willing to let go of it all, even to die, so that we could live in personal pursuit of him, increasingly freed from bondage to all the other things that may control us.

Think of all the anger, anxiety, irritation, impatience, envy, fear, discouragement, obsession, vengeance, bitterness, and violence that result from lesser treasures controlling our hearts. Think how a person's life gets distorted when his job is what he lives for. Think of the bad things that happen when a person becomes the central value in my life. Think of what results when my life is controlled by the quest for a certain position or possession. Why do I get so angry at you? Why do I struggle with impatience? Why am I ever eaten by envy or bitterness? Why would I ever plot vengeance? What would cause me to speak or act unkindly toward you? I don't do these things because you are a flawed person; I do these things because in your flaws, you get in the way of what I treasure. And as long as there is stuff that I have a white-knuckle hold on, you and I will experience conflict. It is only when my heart is owned by Christ that I will be free from the driven and anxious pursuit of things that I cannot properly hold, cannot control, and that will quickly evaporate. Because the big kingdom is a kingdom of sacrifice, it also is a kingdom of freedom.

In order for the kingdom to be a place of glorious new life, it has to be a place of death. Jesus calls you to die to all that you treasure so that he can be the central treasure of your heart. When you value him more than anything else in your life, you are no longer shrinking your life down to what you can hold in your hands and control with your plans. You are beginning to live for something bigger than yourself. When you hold everything in your life with open hands for his taking, you expand everything you touch to the size of his kingdom.

THE FINAL QUESTION: WHOSE KINGDOM ARE YOU MAKING SACRIFICES FOR RIGHT NOW?

WHAT MAKES YOU ANGRY?

CHAPTER SIXTEEN

ANGER

dra·ma: a situation or succession of events in real life having the progression of a play or a story

THE BOTTOM LINE: LIFE IN THE BIG KINGDOM IS ALL ABOUT BEING GOOD AND ANGRY.

I won't soon forget the first time I watched the movie *Magnolia*. Though I would hesitate to recommend it to the average reader of Christian books, it had a gripping plot, interesting characters, confusing details, seemingly contradictory themes, and a multi-thread storyline that developed in unexpected ways. The sin and brokenness portrayed was hard to watch, but it was a captivating drama. As I came to the conclusion of the film, I couldn't believe what I was seeing! My reaction careened back and forth between disappointed shock and confusion. There was one thing for sure: I hadn't really understood the story all along. I couldn't wait until I had the opportunity to watch it again. I have watched *Magnolia* several times since, and I am no longer surprised, because now I understand what the plot is really all about.

The biblical account of the building of the big kingdom is just that shocking of a story. And because it is, it needs to be revisited again and again. It is the greatest drama ever recorded, and it simply cannot be understood in one reading. And so, as we consider what big kingdom living practically looks like, I want to invite you to consider this story with me one more time. I want to invite you to examine the plot in a way you probably have not examined it before. To do so, I want to quote a very familiar passage of Scripture that I am convinced is largely misunderstood. That passage is James 1:19–20. "My dear brothers, take note of this: Everyone should be quick to listen, slow to speak and slow to become angry, for man's anger does not bring about the righteous life that God desires."

THE ANGER CHRONICLES

To fully and practically understand this passage, you have to understand how the Bible operates. The Bible is essentially a narrative, a story. Maybe it would be more accurate to say that the Bible is a theologically annotated story. It is a story with notes for the reader's understanding. James 1:19–20 is not a mechanical life maxim or an isolated biblical principle. This passage is rooted in the plot of the war between the kingdom of God and the kingdom of self. Let me explain further.

The way the Bible is organized is that the main body of content is the unfolding drama of the story of redemption. But as I said before, it is a story with notes. On one side of the narrative are *propositions*. In the propositions, the great themes of the story are distilled down into universal truth statements. The purpose of these statements is to help you understand the plot of the story.

On the other side of the narrative are *principles*. The principles apply the story to the situations and relationships of everyday life. The purpose of the principles is to help you know what it looks like to live within the plot of God's story.

This leads us to James 1:19–20. What you have in this verse is a *principle:* "Everyone should be quick to listen, slow to speak, and slow to become angry," and a *proposition:* "Man's anger does not bring about the righteous life God desires." Let me restate the proposition in a way that is closer to its original form. *"Man's anger does not work God's righteous cause."* When you see the statement in this form, you begin to get clued into what James is actually saying. He is not just saying it's good to be nice and quiet. What he is saying is incredibly more profound than that.

What James is saying is that God's story is an anger story. You could title the biblical story, "The Holy and Unholy War." The narrative of the Bible is really a story of two angers. First is the anger of God. And why is God angry? God is angry because he wants his way—his holy, righteous, perfect, loving way. The second is the anger of people. And why are people angry? We are angry because we want our way—our unholy, selfish, unrighteous, imperfect, unloving way. These two angers cannot coexist. They are mutually exclusive. And as you course your way through the biblical story, encountering both the anger of God and the anger of people, you just know that somehow these two angers are heading for a collision! The Bible really is the chronicle of these two opposing angers.

As you go through the story, you meet the anger of God very early as he drives Adam and Eve out of the garden of Eden. The anger of people runs close behind, unfolding in that shocking moment of sibling homicide as Cain jealously snuffs out Abel's life. The story is marked with the violence of these two angers. You see God's anger against Israel because of Achan's larceny, you see Nebuchadnezzar's anger as he throws the three Israelite young men into that ultraheated furnace, and you see God's anger as he reduces that arrogant monarch to a grazing beast. You watch Israel descend into a social-political quagmire of envy and anger, as king murders king for possession of the throne, and you see God measuring out his anger against his people who have forsaken him for other gods. You see the anger of people in the national infanticide of Herod that accompanies Christ's birth, and you see the anger of God as Christ, in holy fury, goes after those who have turned the house of prayer into a market. These are just a few of the recorded incidents, but they make the point clear. These two angers are at war with one another. There cannot be peace between them.

TWO ANGERS, TWO CAUSES

As the story marches on, you realize that these two kingdoms cannot coexist. God cannot, will not, and must not forsake his righteous cause, his glorious plan. His angry zeal for his righteous cause is the hope of the universe. The hope of the universe is that God will be angry at anything that gets in the way of his cause. His way is the right way. His will must be done.

Yet man seems spiritually incapable of abandoning his cause. He wants what he wants, when he wants it, and in the way he wants it. He holds on with determination to what he has set his heart on. He is not willing to compromise, and he does not want to wait. He is angry at anything or anyone that stands in his way. And his anger is his doom.

What James is saying is that the anger of people has one fatal flaw: it is not motivated by God's righteous cause. Because we do not want what God wants, we are not angry when he is angry and we are angry when he is not. Because we are not motivated by what God is seeking to accomplish, our anger and God's anger do not get along very well.

As you read the biblical story, you can almost feel the drama. You can almost smell the smoke of the war. And you wonder, will God's anger win? Will he give up in disgust and let man have his own selfish way? Will he obliterate us all? Will people ever get it right? Will they ever let go of their selfish cause? Will they ever be angry *with* God, instead of being angry *at* God? How will the story end?

THE COLLISION

As you see the anger of God and the anger of man woven through the biblical story, the dread of the coming collision grips you. And you know that when these two angers collide there is going to be a whole lot of carnage. God wants his holy way, and having his way is the golden hope of the universe. God makes it very clear that he will never abandon his righteous cause. Yet man wants his unholy way and because he demands to have his way, he is in God's way. There simply can be no détente between these two angers.

These two angers do finally collide, but where they collide is unthinkable. They collide in one man. His name is Jesus. Anger explodes in one dramatic moment of violent grace and eternal change on the cross. Listen to the words of Peter's first sermon in Acts 2:22–24.

> Men of Israel, listen to this: Jesus of Nazareth was a man
> accredited by God to you by miracles, wonders and signs, which
> God did among you through him, as you yourselves know.
> This man was handed over to you by God's set purpose and
> foreknowledge; and you, with the help of wicked men, put him
> to death by nailing him to the cross. But God raised him from
> the dead, freeing him from the agony of death, because it was
> impossible for death to keep its hold on him.

What took Christ to the cross? The anger of a holy God who could not tolerate a world of sin and rebellion any longer. This God had planned to express his anger in just this way. But the anger of man also got Christ to the cross. Angry men who wanted their own way and hated the Messiah drove him to the cross. So, on that hill of death, the full anger of God and the full anger of people collided on the back of Christ. He carried the carnage of that collision so that we would never have to carry it again.

This moment of anger did not result in judgment or condemnation, because it was the violent anger of grace. On the cross, Christ was freeing us by grace to give us new life.

GOOD AND ANGRY

What was God seeking to produce by the cross? Was his goal a kingdom of unangry people? No, the cross was meant to produce people who are angry every day. Perhaps you are thinking, "I don't understand. I thought anger was bad and destructive. Doesn't God want us to be peacemakers?"

It is true that most of our anger is dangerous and destructive. This is because it is idolatrous anger. I do not get angry because of your brokenness or the world's brokenness, but because in your brokenness you get in the way of what I crave! On the cross, Christ died to free us from this kind of anger, but not from anger. You see, if you are living for the big kingdom you will be angry *with* God, rather than *at* God.

Jesus died to produce a culture of people who are so in love with him, so committed to his righteous cause, and so distressed by what sin has done to them and their world, that they cannot help but be angry every day. This is not the old, selfish, unholy anger. These people are able to be good *and* angry at the same time.

This new anger is an unquenchable zeal for God's cause and an uncompromising distaste for sin. It is the anger of compassion that cannot help but seek to relieve people who are suffering from sin's damage. It is the anger of mercy that responds to the foolishness of sin with understanding and grace. It is the anger of restoration that refuses to condemn, but believes that lost rebels can be rebuilt into the likeness of Jesus. It is the anger of service that finds delight in helping burdened pilgrims bear their load. It is the anger of peace that hates the division that sin has birthed in our world and does everything that can be done to restore harmony. It is the anger of forgiveness that hates sin's guilt and despises its shame.

Jesus died not only to free you from your anger, but to enable you to take up his righteous anger. He died so that you would not rage inside because people and circumstances loom as constant obstacles to the realization of your little kingdom cravings. He died so that you would not be a captive to the self-absorbed anger of your claustrophobic little kingdom. He died so that you would be angry with sin and the way it has harmed you and everyone around you. He died so that you would be angry at the way sin has damaged the world you live in. He died so that your anger would be holy and pleasing to him. He died so that your anger would propel you to act in deeds of mercy, love, forgiveness, compassion, restoration, and peace.

ANGER: THE BIG AND LITTLE DRAMA

This macro-drama of these two opposing angers, which is played out on the pages of Scripture, is the mini-drama of your life as well. Your response to the situations and relationships of daily life will be shaped by which of these two angers rules your heart. Will you give way to the temptation to fight for your own way? Or, will you grasp the fact that Jesus died for you, not to make your little kingdom work, but to invite you to a better kingdom? Will you take up his righteous cause and express the dissatisfied anger of grace that will cause you to make a difference wherever you are?

Will you be an angry friend, not because your friends, with all their flaws, drive you crazy, but because you see what sin does to them and you want better for them? Will you be an angry spouse, not fighting with your husband or wife, but fighting *for* them as they battle with sin? Will you be an angry citizen, refusing to tolerate poverty, racism, corruption, and injustice? Will you be good *and* angry...

> *when you give yourself to the self-sacrificing anger of love?*
> *when you act with the restorative anger of mercy?*
> *when you respond with rescuing anger of justice?*
> *when you act in the reconciling anger of peace?*

When you are angry in this way, you are no longer a captive to your self-focused dream. Your anger is now the result of taking up God's righteous cause, and you expand everything you touch to the size of God's kingdom.

Sarah is very angry, but she looks anything but angry. She isn't easily irritated. She doesn't have a lot of conflict in her life. She isn't known for being loud and argumentative. But Sarah is angry. She is angry that so many elderly people are institutionalized and alone, so she spends each Sunday afternoon going room to room at the retirement home in her neighborhood. She is angry that in our highly educated culture many inner-city children do not learn to read, so she tutors children on Tuesday night. She is angry that so many friendships end in unreconciled conflict, so she works to be a peacemaker whenever she can. Yes, Sarah is angry, but it's not the self-focused anger of the little kingdom. No, her anger is the anger of the big kingdom and it propels her to look for ways to do good.

THE FINAL QUESTION: RIGHT NOW, WHERE YOU LIVE EVERY DAY, WHOSE KINGDOM DOES YOUR ANGER SERVE?

WHAT IN THE WORLD
GIVES YOU HOPE?

CHAPTER SEVENTEEN

HOPE

*ex·pec·ta·tion: wishing with confidence that
something is about to happen*

THE BOTTOM LINE: TRUE HOPE, THE KIND THAT WILL NEVER DISAPPOINT, IS NEVER HOPE IN A THING, BUT HOPE IN A PERSON.

As I was thinking about this final chapter, I was debating with myself how to properly end our reflection on what big kingdom living looks like. It hit me that the most radical thing about big kingdom living is its hopefulness. The reason you may miss this is because there are so many people who are momentarily motivated by unreliable hope. So, until the source of their hope proves to be unreliable, they function quite hopefully. Because of this it may look like there are more truly hopeful people in this fallen world than there actually are.

When it comes to living with hope in a world that is terribly broken, there are only two classes of people. The first is people who are living in *temporary, soon-to-be disappointed hope.* They have attached their hope to something that will ultimately fail, and so it is just a matter of time before their hope is undone. The second class is people who are living with *valid reason for hope.* Their hope is not facing some impending doom because it has been placed in something that will never disappoint. It is only when you are living for the big kingdom that you have this kind of hope.

DISAPPOINTING DISAPPOINTMENT

Why, you may be asking, is real hope so rare and so radical? Have you taken time to examine the world that you live in? Think about it. There is not much in your life that will not disappoint you in some way. Consider the following real-life example.

Ben and Emily sat before me so incredibly energized and hopeful. They gazed into one another's eyes so intently that it was hard for me to get their attention. In fact, I think there were moments when they forgot that I was in the room. They were in my office for premarital counseling, but I don't think they really thought they needed it. They were jumping through the hoop of counseling so their church would allow them to use their facility for the ceremony. They professed to be deeply respectful and committed to one another. Emily said their communication was excellent, and they had been pretty successful at solving the problems that had come up between them. As Ben and Emily sat tightly together, hand in hand, and with big smiles on their faces, I was afraid for them. They were putting so much of their personal sense of well-being, meaning, security, and hope in the assurance that the other person would pull it off. Their hope rested in the belief that the other person would not disappoint them.

Six months later they were in my office again, but this time Ben and Emily were not sitting so close. The smiles on their faces were gone. They had faced the shocking reality that each was a sinner married to a sinner. They had made poor choices and experienced broken promises. Unresolved conflicts had left a legacy of hurt that now made their communication difficult. Their issues weren't huge. They were the garden-variety weeds of life in a fallen world. But the thing that stood out to me was that their hope for their still-young marriage was gone.

DISAPPOINTING WORLD, RADICAL HOPE

This once-hopeful couple had reason for disappointment. There had been failure. Things hadn't turned out as they had imagined. They did have problems to deal with. You see, the music of life in this broken world is often played in a minor key, because it is the music of disappointment. Think about it for a moment. There is almost nothing you have been involved with that hasn't disappointed you in some way. That house you bought has proven to have problems that you never anticipated. Every friendship you've ever had has disappointed you in some way. Your job hasn't always left you encouraged and excited. When you first began to attend your church, perhaps you thought it was the greatest church ever. Now you've been involved long enough to bump into many of its flaws, and your appraisal is much more realistic. You were raised in a family where disappointment was a normal reality. Such is life in a fallen world. In fact, it is accurate to say that disappointment is the universal experience of every human being, and sadness is the emotion that no person has ever escaped. Because of this it needs to be said that one of the most radical things about the big kingdom of God is that it is a kingdom of bright, shining, personally motivating, eternal hope. The hope of this kingdom rests on something that is so utterly fixed and secure that it will never, ever disappoint.

SO WHAT'S UP WITH HOPE?

Have you ever wondered why no one has ever written a book on how to become depressed? Why no one has ever written a book on the seven best ways to become fearful? Or why no one has ever written "Seven Steps to a Highly Effective Life of Disappointment"? None of these books has been written because they simply haven't been necessary. Life in this terribly broken world is hard. It often feels like for every step forward you take three steps back. Sometimes it seems like just as you are about to realize your dreams, they evaporate before your very eyes. Often it looks like the bad guys are winning and the good guys just keep on getting hammered. There are moments when it seems like crime pays and honesty doesn't make good on its debts. When you take a long look at what is happening around you, it really isn't stupid to conclude that hope is the dedicated occupation of fools.

But open up your mind, put down your fear for a moment, and think with me. If you're married, admit it, you have not been summarily happy with every aspect of your spouse or with everything your marriage has experienced. For all the joys and blessings, there are ways that your marriage has been a struggle, even right up to this moment. Or think about your job. It has disappointed you. Perhaps it's your relationship with your boss. You seemed to connect and complement so well at first, but now there are tensions that you really don't understand. Or perhaps it's your fellow workers. You feel like you are more in a competition with them than a community. Or maybe it's the work itself. Perhaps it never became as engaging and fulfilling as you imagined it would be.

There has never been a parent who isn't disappointed in some way. We dream of what it will be like to have children, and we dream about how they will turn out. But, we never realize our dreams. Our children struggle in ways that we never foresaw, and we struggle with our children in ways that we would have thought impossible before they were born. Somewhere in the process the old idealism withers, and we all just hope we can survive the process and still love one another.

Or maybe you have hit the wall with the friendships around you. Perhaps you're incredibly lonely and you wonder if anyone really cares for you. Or maybe you're hurt because some professed friend has betrayed you. Maybe you are tired of relationships that are surface-y and meaningless, never getting down to the level where real friendship should always hang out. Or maybe the disappointment is with yourself. Perhaps you seem all-too-skilled at doing the wrong thing at the wrong time, robbing promising friendships of their future. For every one of us, our experience of friendship has been disappointing in some way.

It could be that the biggest disappointment in your life is your church. You read in the Bible what the church could be, but it never seems to achieve that. There are lots of fellowship and ministry opportunities, but it all seems like a poorly designed system of pseudo-spiritual busyness. You've participated at every level, but there is something missing.

It is possible that your biggest disappointment in life is you. You have never been the person you wanted to be or accomplished what you wanted to accomplish. In your quiet and logical moments, you know you have no one to blame but yourself. You let yourself off the hook when you should have held yourself accountable. You blamed others when you should have shouldered the responsibility yourself. And you were all too able to rationalize your poor performance by citing the tough situations around you. When you have moments of self-insight, it's hard not to be disappointed with the you that you have become.

Yes sir, there are lots of reasons to be discouraged. There are lots of things to fear. None of us has lived a life free of disappointment. In light of this, one of the most radical things about the big kingdom of God is that it is a kingdom of bright, shining, eternal hope.

DISAPPOINTING HOPE

There is an important big kingdom principle that Paul lays out almost surreptitiously in Romans 5:1–5.

> Therefore, since we have been justified through faith, we have peace with God through our Lord Jesus Christ, through whom we have gained access by faith into this grace in which we now stand. And we rejoice in the hope of the glory of God. Not only so, but we also rejoice in our sufferings, because we know that suffering produces perseverance; perseverance, character; and character, hope. And hope does not disappoint us, because God has poured out his love into our hearts by the Holy Spirit, whom he has given us.

Paul is celebrating the implications of God's accepting grace on our daily lives. He says that God's grace even gives us reason to be hopeful right in the middle of suffering. Often suffering is the very thing that removes our hope, but not for Paul. What gives Paul hope is not that the situations and relationships of his life are easy and working well. No, his hope lives at a deeper level. That is how he is able to retain his hope even when he finds himself in circumstances that are both difficult and painful.

It is at this point of the discussion that Paul slips in this subtle, but explosive principle. Here it is. If your hope disappoints you, it is the wrong kind of hope. You see, hope in God never disappoints, precisely because it is hope *in God*. This means that hope placed in any other thing will always end up disappointing. Let this principle sink in for a moment. Allow yourself to consider how far-reaching and life-altering its implications are.

What do we mean when we say we are hoping for something? Essentially, hope is a *desire coupled with a logical or confident expectation of fulfillment*. But hope is much more than this. When I place my hope in something, I am attaching my sense of well-being, identity, meaning, and purpose to that thing in some way. In this way I *"need"* my hopes to become realities because I have connected my life to them. You must realize that every human being does this. If you are still alive and able to think and feel, you are putting your hope somewhere. Some kind of hope gets every person out of bed in the morning. This is also why disappointment is such a universal human experience, because most of what we hope in isn't able to deliver. So we keep shuffling our little deck of hope cards, thinking that sooner or later we will come up with an ace. But the deck we're holding doesn't have any aces in it! *When your hope disappoints you, it is because it is the wrong hope.*

ANOTHER WAY

But hope does have another way. Big kingdom living is living with guarantees. God's kingdom *will* come. It's my kingdom that won't. His will *will* be done. There is a good chance that mine won't. He will bring all things to a glorious conclusion. Every promise he has ever made will be fulfilled. Everything we have encountered, experienced, and endured has a goal to it. There will be a final accounting. An actual time is coming when evil will be once and for all defeated. All of God's children will attend the funeral of death, because death is going to die. Mercy will reign forever. The meek will, in fact, inherit the earth. Peace will live forever and ever. There will be a real day when suffering, sorrow, sin, and pain will end.

The problem is that when you elevate your little kingdom desires to "needs," you no longer live with guarantees. But God has not promised to deliver all the things you have hoped, desired, and convinced yourself that you cannot live without. You have attached your happiness to a deeply romantic marriage, but God hasn't promised to give you one. You have connected your identity to a long and successful career, but God has not promised to deliver it. You have glued your well-being to your physical or material health, but God hasn't guaranteed you either one of them. You have placed your value in being a successful parent with trophy children, but God has not contracted to deliver your family dream. Of course these things are all wonderful to desire and worthwhile to experience, but they are out of your control, and your Redeemer has not guaranteed to give them to you.

Further, when these things control your heart and command your hopes, you will tend to judge God's faithfulness, not by whether he has been true to his promises, but by whether he has given you the things that you have set your heart on. But this is right where the redemptive quandary lies. If God gives you the things that are playing a role in your life that only he is supposed to play, wouldn't he be encouraging in you the very addictions from which his grace is meant to free you?

In fact, I am convinced that much of the resistance we attribute to the enemy is actually the resistance of the Lord. He stands against us, not because he doesn't love us, but because he *does* love us. He stands in our way because what we want is spiritually in the way of what *he* wants for us.

The brand of Christianity that presents God as the ultimate guarantor of our felt needs always becomes hopeless and self-defeating. You see, we struggle with hopelessness and doubt because the "good" things we want seem constantly beyond our reach. The irony is that we are already receiving the best things from his hands, but we don't even recognize it.

Your hope is absolutely attached to what kingdom you are serving. If your life is defined by how many of your little kingdom purposes you can realize, you will tend to be stressed, controlling, anxious, disappointed, and fearful. You have defined your life by what you cannot control and by what God has not promised. Sadly, it is all very self-defeating. But if your hope no longer rests on your personal wisdom, strength, and character, if it no longer rests on the acceptance and performance of other people, and no longer rests on the belief that circumstances, institutions, and situations will not fail you, then you are beginning to move toward reliable hope.

Big kingdom hope rests on one place and one place alone—God. It is the deeply held and daily acted-upon trust that God is the ultimate source of all that is wise, true, loving, and good, that what he is doing is best, and that what he has promised is reliable. The only hope that will not disappoint is hope in a Person. Big kingdom hope is about entrusting my past, present and future, my identity, meaning and purpose, and my motivation for daily functioning to God and resting unafraid in him. Sure, I will still face the disappointments of life in this fallen world. But, I will not panic, I will not run, and I will not quit, because my God is present even in my disappointment, and he will never change!

When you wake up with this kind of hope, when it shapes how you deal with people and circumstances, when your hope really is in God and God alone, you expand everything you touch to the size of his kingdom.

Each morning that greets me is full of hope,
Not because I am successful at what I am doing,
Or because the people near me appreciate me,
Or because circumstances are easy,
But because God is and he is my Father.
To look at the morning in any other way
Is to believe a lie.
To live in hope is to live in truth;
To live in truth is to bring Him glory;
To bring God glory in my daily living
Is the highest form of worship. (PDT)

THE FINAL QUESTION: WHERE DO YOU TEND TO LOOK FOR DAILY HOPE?

CHAPTER EIGHTEEN

PUTTING IT ALL TOGETHER

Zack is engaged. I don't mean in the romantic sense. I mean in the sense that he is involved. On the surface, Zack's life looks pretty ordinary. He lives in the city and is the manager of a local grocery store. He has a tight circle of friends with whom he stays in close contact. He is very involved with the church in his neighborhood. Zack is thirty-one and not yet married, although there is a woman in his life.

When I say that Zack is engaged, I mean that the way he lives is a concrete example of what this book is all about. Zack gets it; he gets what it means to expand his life to the size of God's kingdom. No, that doesn't necessarily mean he's going to quit his job and go to some remote country as a missionary. You really can live for God's kingdom right where you are. In fact, that is exactly what God has called you and given you the grace to do. Let's look at Zack's life a little more closely.

Zach is in the city because the largest concentration of people is there. Zack is excited about the fact that in the city there are loads of public space that he shares with scores of other people every day. This provides him with natural opportunities to greet and eventually meet people he would not otherwise know. And why does he want to do this? Because he is serious about God's call to be salt and light in the place where God has put him. He is excited about the opportunities that he has every day to incarnate the love of the Lord Jesus Christ.

If you were to walk the streets with Zack, you would be convinced that he knows everyone in his neighborhood. He is never too busy or self-absorbed to stop and say hello. After his MBA, Zack purposely looked for a job in his neighborhood that would put him in daily contact with the people in his neighborhood. All of the regular shoppers at the store know Zack.

Zack is known for his willingness to help. He regularly takes care of his neighbor's boxer. The dog is too big for Zack's condo and slobbers a lot, but he has also provided an opportunity for Zack to be engaged in the life of the career-driven couple who live next door. He has also become a surrogate son to the elderly lady down the street. Without Zack, her sidewalks would never be shoveled in the winter, and he regularly delivers her groceries to her.

Saturday morning is Zack's time in the neighborhood park. Yes, he needs to exercise and is concerned about staying fit as he gets older, but there is more going on here. The touch football and three-on-three basketball games at the park have enabled Zack to get to know lots of the young guys in his neighborhood. Although it would be more efficient for Zack to join a gym, he has bigger reasons for staying in the park.

In the summers, Zack does everything he can to make his deck barbecue central, inviting someone to have a meal with him almost every weekend. Zack is a natural evangelist, but not in a forced, button-holing way. By the time Zack begins to talk about his relationship with Christ, the people around him are already attracted to who he is, and they already wonder what makes him tick.

WHEN THE BIG KINGDOM MEETS THE SIDEWALK

Zack lives the way he does for one reason: he has his eyes on the big kingdom. He could be living in a bigger place. He could have a more prestigious, better paying job. He could own nicer things and have much more free time to himself. He could have all of these things, but he chooses not to because Zack isn't living for Zack. Zack really loves living for the King. Here are the foundation stones of what that means.

Zack believes in the importance of place. He believes that the sovereign King of the universe has put him exactly where he wants him. And that means he should love the people in it and do everything he can to make it a better place.

Zack believes in ministry as a lifestyle. Most Christians make the mistake of thinking about ministry in a formal sense. They think of ministry as a program that is scheduled. In this model, you step out of your life into ministry, and then out of ministry back into your life. Zack believes that life is ministry, that every dimension of human life is at once a forum for ministry.

Zack believes in the redemptive power of relationships. Zack believes the Bible's teaching that redemptive activity always takes place in the context of relationships. This is how God works in our lives. Through Christ, he accepts us into loving relationship with him, and then he goes to work to radically change us. So Zack looks for every opening he can find to build relationships with the people around him.

Zack believes in the importance of hospitality. Just as God opens the doors of his family to him, Zack believes he makes a very powerful statement when he opens the doors of his private world to the people that God has placed near him.

Zack believes that he is called to live with patience and perseverance. Ministry is always a process and not an event. Ministry is the willingness to make long-term investments in the lives of others, with the hope that God will do what he alone can do as we are making those investments. As Zack commits himself to a long-term investment in loving others, he reminds himself of the patience with which he has been treated by his heavenly Father.

Because Zack is living this way, everything he does is bigger than it seems. Work has expanded to the size of God's kingdom. Walking to work becomes more than walking to work; it, too, becomes kingdom work. Things as mundane as exercise and barbecuing take on new significance because even they are part of Zack's living large.

Sure, there are times when Zack goes out to eat just to have a good meal or goes to a movie simply for the sake of entertainment. But even these activities Zack holds with an open hand, always ready for God to alter the plan.

WHAT DOES IT MEAN FOR YOU?
SOME PERSONAL QUESTIONS

As you are now near the end of this book, it's important for you to use it as a mirror. Looking at yourself through the truths of this book, what do you see? What kingdom shapes your decisions and sets your schedule? Have you shrunk your life to the size of your life, or have you expanded everything you are doing to the size of God's kingdom? These final questions are designed to help you accurately evaluate your lifestyle, and my hope is that they will produce in you a quest for more.

1. Are you doing the concrete things in your life regularly because you are living for something bigger than your own personal definition of happiness?

2. Do you live aware of the deceptive nature of the kingdom of self (remember, it really is a costume kingdom), regularly examining your motives and how you are investing your time and energy?

3. Are you living that form-and-freedom *jazz* life that God has called you to? Are you committed to staying within the boundaries of what he has written, yet enjoying the freedom to improvise in the situations and relationships where he has placed you?

4. Are you dissatisfied with the broken world that you live and work in every day? And do you work for its restoration to wholeness in any way you can?

5. Have you allowed yourself to be so busy with work on earth that you do not have time to long for heaven? Or is everything you do done with one eye on the present and one eye on eternity? Are you able to deal with the pain and disappointment of today because you really have embraced the promise of a day when this world and everything in it will be made completely new?

6. Do you hold loosely to your plans, your schedule, your agenda, your expectations? Are you always looking for ways to be part of what God is doing wherever you are, no matter how mundane the moment is?

7. Do you live with a deep appreciation for the Lord Jesus Christ and the gift of grace that has fundamentally changed you and the course of your life? Do you work to keep your love and worship of him fresh and new? Do you live with a sense of humble privilege that not only have you been chosen to be a citizen of his kingdom, but his ambassador as well?

We were never made or remade to live for ourselves. We were created for transcendence. The borders of our lives were always meant to be way bigger than the borders of our lives. When we live this way, by his grace, we not only become part of the most important work in the universe, but we are given back our humanity. This is the way every human being was designed to live! Though God is infinitely patient, he will never accept our little kingdom purposes. Since he loves us so, he will again and again reach into our claustrophobic little kingdoms of one and pry us out. And he will keep doing this until his will is finally done and his kingdom has finally come. Now that is a reason for celebration!

NOTES

Chapter 3: A Total Disaster

1. Jim Collins, *Good to Great* (New York: Harper Collins, 2001), p. 1.

Chapter 5: Discovering Your Civilization

1. David W. Henderson, *Culture Shift* (Grand Rapids: Baker Books, 1998), pp. 29–30.

Chapter 6: The Costume Kingdom

1. Vinoth Ramachandra, *Gods that Fail* (Downers Grove, IL: InterVarsity Press, 1997), pp. 40–41.
2. Ibid., pp. 41–42.

Chapter 7: The Shrink Dynamic

1. C.S. Lewis, *Mere Christianity* (San Francisco: Zondervan/Harper, 2001), p. 118.